PENNY STOCKS

A Complete Guide to Make Money Online,
Trading on the Penny Stock Market

(Fundamental Skills to Dominate Penny Stocks)

Patricia White

Published by Kevin Dennis

Patricia White

All Rights Reserved

Penny Stocks: A Complete Guide to Make Money Online, Trading on the Penny Stock Market (Fundamental Skills to Dominate Penny Stocks)

ISBN 978-1-989965-63-4

All rights reserved. No part of this guide may be reproduced in any form without permission in writing from the publisher except in the case of brief quotations embodied in critical articles or reviews.

Legal & Disclaimer

The information contained in this book is not designed to replace or take the place of any form of medicine or professional medical advice. The information in this book has been provided for educational and entertainment purposes only.

The information contained in this book has been compiled from sources deemed reliable, and it is accurate to the best of the Author's knowledge; however, the Author cannot guarantee its accuracy and validity and cannot be held liable for any errors or omissions. Changes are periodically made to this book. You must consult your doctor or get professional medical advice before using any of the suggested remedies, techniques, or information in this book.

Upon using the information contained in this book, you agree to hold harmless the Author from and against any damages, costs, and expenses, including any legal fees potentially resulting from the application of any of the information provided by this guide. This disclaimer applies to any damages or injury caused by the use and application, whether directly or indirectly, of any advice or information presented, whether for breach of contract, tort, negligence, personal injury, criminal intent, or under any other cause of action.

You agree to accept all risks of using the information presented inside this book. You need to consult a professional medical practitioner in order to ensure you are both able and healthy enough to participate in this program.

Table of Contents

INTRODUCTION 1

CHAPTER 1: TAKING THE FIRST STEP 8

CHAPTER 2: THE RISKS AND BENEFITS 15

CHAPTER 3: UNDERSTANDING WHAT A PENNY STOCK IS 28

CHAPTER 4: FINDING YOUR TRADING STYLE..................... 32

CHAPTER 5: HOW TO GET STARTED WITH PENNY STOCKS 47

CHAPTER 6: TACTICS AND STRATEGY............................... 63

CHAPTER 7: MANAGING RISK AND UNDERSTANDING YOUR PROFITABILITY.. 71

CHAPTER 8: THE HABIT OF MANAGING YOUR EMOTIONS AT ALL TIMES... 83

CHAPTER 9: UNDERSTANDING THE PSYCHOLOGY OF TRADING AND HOW IT AFFECTS YOU 87

CHAPTER 10: TECHNIQUES FOR MAKING MONEY WITH PENNY STOCKS 93

CHAPTER 11: HOW PENNY STOCKS PRICES VARY 104

CHAPTER 12: TRADING PENNY STOCKS 116

CHAPTER 13: GENERAL TRENDS IN STOCK TRADING...... 133

CHAPTER 14: MAKING WISE PENNY STOCK CHOICES..... 139

CHAPTER 15: THE STEPS TO SUCCESS IN PENNY STOCKS 146

CHAPTER 16: HOW STOCK SCREENERS HELP YOU TRADE PENNY STOCKS 158

CHAPTER 17: TO BUSINESS - PENNY STOCKS BASICS 164

CHAPTER 18: PENNY STOCK FAQS 173

CHAPTER 19: HOW TO GET THE MOST OUT OF PENNY STOCKS 180

CONCLUSION 187

Introduction

The stock market is a vast place where thousands of transactions take place every day, all over the world. Most of us have a vague idea of what it is and how it works, but few people really understand it and how to work with it. This book is aimed to help you become one of those few people.

Stock markets are physical places where buyers and sellers converge daily to buy and sell stocks and other financial securities in order to capitalize upon their ever-changing values. There are many types of financial securities that people can invest in, with the most preferred ones being stocks.

Stocks or shares are part of a company, which are issued to the public on a regular basis. There are many types of stocks such as ordinary, preferred, and penny stocks. In this book, we will look at the last type in detail to understand what penny stocks stand for.

This book is a complete and thorough guide to penny stocks and penny stock trading. While penny stock trading can be complicated, as can any type of stock trading, this book will provide you with the information necessary for you to understand penny stock trading and will leave you ready to start trading in penny stocks once you have completed the entire book.

We will take you from the basics of defining penny stocks and associated concepts so that you understand the basic terminology and concepts of penny stock trading before getting more in depth into the topic.

Then we will move into how to get started in penny stock trading, where you will be given information about the basic resources that you need to be properly prepared to trade in penny stocks.

After that, we will discuss how the prices of penny stocks are calculated. Valuation and share price are complicated concepts, with a variety of factors that come into play, and this book will take you through those various factors and explain how each impacts the price of a penny stock.

Once you understand the basics of penny stock pricing, we will move into how to select the penny stocks in which you are going to invest. This section will look at factors to consider when choosing both the company and the specific stocks in which you will be investing. There are several criteria to consider when determining whether a penny stock is the right investment opportunity for you.

The next chapter goes through an extensive and in-depth examination of the various ways in which the price of penny stocks can be predicted. There are a number of methods and they can seem quite complicated. However, after reading through this section you will have a clear understanding of the different methods, the data that they provide, and how you can use them to make your investment decisions.

Next, we will look at the analysis methods for penny stocks. This includes analysis of a company's fundamentals, such as the income statement, balance sheet, and cash flow statement. It also includes an alternative analysis method, the technical analysis, which examines a company's share price patterns and trends. All of these analysis techniques are useful and they should be used in conjunction with each other when determining which penny stocks you are interested in purchasing.

Then we will look at day trading, what it is, and why you should day-trade in penny stocks. While some people may think that day trading is not appropriate for penny stocks, this section will explain that it certainly can be appropriate, and why it might be the right decision for you.

After this is an examination of the dos and don'ts of penny stocks: What you absolutely should do and what you should avoid if you are going to start trading in penny stocks. Dos include creating an investment plan and making investment rules for yourself, while don'ts include getting caught up in investment schemes and expecting to become rich overnight. This section has a lot of general but practical information that will help you to successfully invest in penny stocks.

We will then move into myths and FAQs of penny stocks and clear up some common misunderstandings that you may also have about penny stocks and penny stock trading. We will also review the advantages and disadvantages of penny stocks so that you have a clear idea of what you can and cannot expect from trading in penny stocks.

The next chapter will go through some important terminologies that you will need to know and understand in order to successfully navigate the world of penny stocks. These terminologies are applicable not only to penny stock trading but to trading in higher-value stocks, as well.

Then we will discuss the different types of trade exchanges, market traders, and market indices, which will give you a clear understanding of the trading system and how to operate within it. After that, we will look at the various kinds of brokers and promoters you might encounter during your ventures into the world of penny stock trading, and will discuss which of these can be helpful to you and which are best avoided.

Finally, we will end with the most important rules to follow when investing in penny stocks, including carrying out comprehensive and proper research and implementing damage control as soon as possible if you discover that you have made a bad decision. These rules, if you follow them, will play a significant role in allowing you to earn profits and avoid losses. The last section of the book is a summary of the key highlights of the book and is a useful section to return to remind yourself of essential concepts and ideas about penny stock trading.

Many people view penny stocks are a very risky investment. You may have heard people say that trading in the stock market is like gambling. For the uninformed investor, this may be the case, but if you do your homework, inform yourself, and understand how the market works, penny stock trading can become a very lucrative hobby or means of building capital. Reading this book will help calm your nerves and let you understand better how to invest money without experiencing what we all fear - losing it all.

Once you have read all of the sections and are sure that you understand the information provided, you will be fully prepared to enter the world of penny stock trading and start making your investment decisions. Then the next step will be up to you. Which penny stocks will you choose? There is only one way to find out: read this book, and then get started on investing!

Chapter 1: Taking The First Step

If you are reading this book, you have decided to dive into the world of trading. Before you move forward, however, you should keep in mind that stocks, especially penny stock investments, are not for everyone. Immersing yourself in the world of penny stocks and investing requires varying degrees of financial risk, and high levels of personal patience. If you are willing to invest your money and time into this type of activity, however, this book will help you get started.

Like we mentioned earlier, penny stocks trading is a perfect opportunity for beginner traders, primarily because a vast number of companies offer and sell stocks for low prices—stock prices range from a penny to $5.00 a share, which is the traditional ending price for a penny stock. These "penny" prices are more often than not associated with young or small companies, companies that have been recently established or, for varying reasons, struggle to achieve gradual or efficient growth in business. However, penny stocks are also sold by bigger and older companies whose prices are around and above $5.00 a share. A large number of people are attracted to penny stocks trading because of these low prices. For someone who is just stepping into the world of trading, this type of stock is the perfect choice for that reason.

Penny stocks investments are oftentimes alluring financial prospects because of the possibility of high returns—you can invest a small amount of money but potentially make a large return and profit. This is great for the investor who can't afford to invest in big stocks, or for those who don't know or understand the more complicated and advanced trading strategies.

Penny stocks are also great investment opportunities because they're rather easy to purchase and allow you to easily manage up to 1,000 shares. It wasn't always like this in the past, however. In past years, no one would have bought or sold a stock for more than $0.25 a share. Nowadays, on the other hand, electronic trading is expensive and penny stocks are considered to be rather cheap. There are still those out there, however, that continue to write off the value of penny stocks. In fact, there are investors that still believe that penny stocks are a fluke and shouldn't be invested in because their price is less than $5.00 per share, and therefore, only struggling or non-prosperous companies sell them. Everyone has their own opinion on the subject, but, as you'll hopefully soon discover, penny stock investments can be quite advantageous and profitable.

Reaping the benefits from a penny stock is not a hard task to achieve because you simply need a small increase in a penny stock's price to see financial growth. For example, a doubling—a full 100% return on your investment—can occur if the stock goes from just $1 to $2. It's a small increase that has the potential to bring with it rather large growth margins. In contrast, if a $25 stock increases by a dollar, the increase in the percentage will only be between 2% and 4%. Both of these scenarios are real occurrences in the penny stock market, so you can see just how unpredictable and wide-ranging the characteristics and outcomes of penny stock trading can be.

Penny stock investment opportunities can oftentimes be found in resource fields and industries including the medical field, silver and gold mining industries, and oil development. Your investments should generally be in fields that interest you, so if these industries don't spark your interest, don't worry. Penny stock investment opportunities can be found in many other industries as well. A quick search on the internet will answer any lingering questions you have on this topic.

Before we move forward, keep in mind that penny stocks are sometimes referred to as "micro-cap stocks" because of the size they have in their market capitalization. Think of it this way: if you sell a stock for $2.00 a share and that stock has 4 million shares, this makes the total market capitalization $8 million. As a bonus to their low price and high potential for market capitalization, you can find penny stocks trading at low volumes with rather dramatic price volatility.

Yes, penny stocks can certainly be very profitable, but they do sometimes pose a risk to future growth and investments, especially for young companies. Penny stock investments can be risky for a beginner because there are many stock promoters operating in this financial arena who have no qualms about taking advantage of less-experienced investors. This, unfortunately, is what all too often gives a negative reputation to penny stocks and the otherwise advantageous investment opportunities they have to offer.

Today, penny stocks can be found in over-the-counter markets. The stocks in these markets are less liquid and don't require a lot to remain listed. Many of the companies that offer and sell these stocks don't file annual financial reports, which is why their stocks can be easily managed by people with less experience. The stocks that come from these particular companies can be quite risky, however, though this doesn't mean that there aren't plenty of other safe and reliable penny stocks available in the marketplace. Actually, there are plenty of safe penny stocks backed by trusted products and services that will meet the financial needs and personal interests of consumers and investors alike. These trustworthy and reliable stocks can be found in industries that are constantly and gradually growing, have experienced, knowledgeable teams, and are founded upon effective trading strategies and strategic marketing plans that will produce growth. Before you begin trading in penny stocks, however, you'll want to make sure that you've done enough research—not just about the topic of penny stocks, but also about the available penny stocks in the market. That is, to be profitable in the field of penny stocks, you'll need to know how to choose the most profitable investment opportunities.

For the inexperienced investor, penny stock investments may turn out to be poor investments choices for a variety of reasons. The trick to avoiding this, though, is to identify the profitable penny stocks from the unconducive ones in the marketplace. You'll be able to tell a profitable penny stock from an unprofitable one by determining its likelihood of future growth and estimating its percentage return on your investment. It sounds a bit complicated, though, does it not? After all, how can an inexperienced investor determine the likelihood of future growth and estimate percentage return? Well, fortunately, we'll address the different, reliable sources of information and approaches that contain the qualified and required knowledge and formulas to do just this in the following chapter.

Chapter 2: The Risks And Benefits

Investing in penny stocks can either be very rewarding or disappointing. It has a potential to make some serious profit within a short period of time, but there is also a high probability of losing all your investment just as fast.

Your objective as an investor, of course, is to turn that potential profit into a reality. Unfortunately, the majority of those who invest in penny stocks end up disappointed. Although it remains tempting to make an investment, you should know the risks that you will be facing.

The risks

Bankruptcy

There are two kinds of companies that are active in the penny stock market:

Small or start-up companies

Companies that are about to go bankrupt

Small or start-up companies can either grow or soon close down. If it grows, then you would be happy about your investment. But, if it fails to earn a decent amount of profit, you will either earn an insignificant amount or lose your investment. Unfortunately, the penny stock market also has many companies that are struggling to survive. You should avoid investing in these companies. However, companies that are going bankrupt would usually hide such fact. Instead, they usually project a nice image to tempt people to make an investment, with a hope that the funds they will collect can save the company from bankruptcy. Therefore, before placing any investment, be sure to make a thorough research and analysis of the company concerned.

Of course, struggling companies can still do well in the long run. However, this is a very risky investment. When you invest in penny stocks, you become a common stockholder. As such, you will not exercise any control over the assets of the company, not even how these assets will be used or distributed. When a company finally declares bankruptcy and it does not have enough assets to pay its debts (which is something that usually happens), all its assets will be sold, and you will receive nothing. It is a zero game for you. So, since you have other more feasible options where to put your money in, it would be better if you just avoid those companies that are struggling to survive and just stick to those companies that are actually doing well.

Start-up companies

The penny stock market is a haven for new and start-up companies. Since you will encounter many start-up companies, you will only be able to gather a little information about its history. Therefore, it would be difficult to tell whether it is a legitimate company or simply a group that wants to snatch away your money. Yes, there are many scammers out there, so you should be careful about making any investment. And, since you will be dealing with small companies, and small companies do not get as much attention as big and well-established enterprises, mismanagement by the executives of the company may become an issue, where the high executives view the company assets as their own personal property and do not acknowledge the ownership of the stockholders, which includes penny stockholders.

Less transparent

Unlike blue-chip stocks, penny stocks do not have a strict requirement primarily because of their low value. They are usually traded over the counter (OTC) or on the Pink Sheets. The Pink Sheets is privately owned and does not have any centralized trading floor. OTC means that the stocks are traded in an environment that is not centralized or formal and is not strictly regulated. The Pink Sheets is also considered an OTC.

Companies that you can find on the Pink Sheets are not required to file anything with the SEC, and they are not required to observe the minimum capital stock. Therefore, it is hard to get details about these companies. And, be careful because many scammers join the Pink Sheets. Most companies on the Pink Sheets either want to hide their true information or are simply so small that they cannot meet the minimum capitalization requirement.

Low liquidity

The low liquidity level of penny stocks makes it difficult to sell. It also makes it prone to fraudulent schemes like the pump and dump. As the term implies, the value of certain penny stocks is pumped using a fraudulent marketing hype to make them look attractive to investors. Once the investors buy them, they get dumped—their prices will begin to drop dramatically simply because their true value is far less than how they were promoted. The result: The investor is at a loss.

Keep in mind that the pump and dump scheme can also be applied even when the company is actually growing well. In fact, this makes it more convincing, because there are real factors that exist that can make you believe and even rationalize the increase in the price of the company's penny stocks. When the company is doing well, by adding even just a dollar, it would be difficult to tell if such increase is due to an actually improving stock value, which is legitimate, or a mere pump and dump scheme.

Speculative

The penny stock market is said to be speculative for good reasons. There are so many factors that affect the prices of penny stocks, and these factors which are outside your control must work together in your favor for you to make a decent amount of profit.

Despite the many schemes out there, you need to be able to identify good and profitable penny stocks. Even if you have chosen a good set of stocks, it is up to the company to improve and the market must respond accordingly. And even if the value of your penny stocks increases, there is no guarantee that it will continue to increase to yield a significant profit. Should you finally decide to sell them, will they still look like an attractive investment? Who would be willing to buy them?

These risks, among others, are faced by penny stock traders and investors. Although a good investment can give you a big return, the majority of people who invest in penny stocks lose their investment.

Now, do you still think that this is a good investment? Are you honestly up for the challenge? If yes, then it is time for you to find out the benefits of investing in penny stocks.

The Benefits

Venturing into the penny stock market is a challenging adventure. If you think that your entrepreneurial spirit is strong enough, then welcome to a place of high rewards and high profits. This is where you can double, triple, and even make your investment grow more than 10 times its original value. If you want to be cautious, you can just start low and watch the value soar within a short period of time. It is true that investing in penny stocks is not for everyone. If you are up for the challenge and the risks involved, then this can give you that financial freedom you have always wanted.

Affordable

A single penny stock is only worth less than $5. Therefore, this is an investment that you can do even if you are on a tight budget. Although the stake may be small, its profit potential remains high.

High return

The companies that issue penny stocks are usually the small, start-up companies. This is means that there is so much space for improvements. As these companies improve, their penny stock value also increases. This is another reason why penny stocks can give you a higher return than blue-chip stocks. Blue-chip stocks are already stable and usually experience only small and slow fluctuations in value. When you enter the penny stock market, you would not be surprised to see the prices of certain stocks to double their value within a short period of time. And what is more, some can even increase to more than 20 times their initial value.

Low or controlled losses

Since penny stocks have a low cost, your losses (if any) will be minimized. And, if you invest in different penny stocks, you will encounter some losses, but you will also realize some profit from certain penny stocks that you have invested in. In fact, even if you randomly invest in different kind of penny stocks, it would not be surprising that some of those stocks will make you money. But, of course, due to carelessness and lack of research, you will probably end up with more losses than profits.

High volume

Because penny stocks are so cheap, you can buy many stocks even if you only have a small capital. In fact, many people who simply want to test the water begin with a capital of less than $1,000. Still, some of these starters are able to double, triple, and even make it grow well that they no longer need to add additional funds to their account. Moreover, since penny stocks are very affordable, you can easily diversify your investment by getting different kinds of penny stocks.

Chapter 3: Understanding What A Penny Stock Is

A penny stock is a stock of a small company which is traded at a low price per share. The SEC of the United States of America defines the penny stock as a tradable security worth below $5 per share. This stock isn't traded in major exchanges and doesn't meet some criteria. On the other hand, a penny stock in the United Kingdom is a stock which traded below£1 per share. Because it is low priced, the company which offers the penny stock has low capitalization and is very volatile. This stock can also be easily manipulates through pump and dump schemes. Therefore, a lot of investors are often duped into investing in it. In the United States of America, the penny stocks are transacted over-the-counter through Pink Sheets or OTC Bulletin Board. The sale of a penny stock is regulated by the

Financial Industry Regulatory Authority and the SEC.

Trading of a penny stock isn't as liquid as the major stocks trading. Stock manipulators and promoters can easily come up with fraudulent strategies to make it appear that a particular penny stock is heavily traded. What these people usually do is buy a large chunk of the penny stock shares then they artificially inflate the price by coming up with strategies to mislead new prospective investors. They issue newsletters. They create interest about the penny stock in message boards and chat rooms. Furthermore, they issue fake press releases and send email blasts. They claim to have inside information about the stock. Once a lot of unsuspecting new investors become interested in the penny stock, they sell their inventory at a high price. The internet and devices are often used to perpetrate the scam. Rapper 50 Cent turned to Twitter to inflate the price of HNHI. He was reported to have earned

$8.7 million from the sale of his 30 million penny stock shares after his Twitter post. Another company, Lithium Exploration Group didn't have any assets reported in its form 10-Q in 2010 but through its direct mail campaign it was able to raise at least $350 million. It later acquired lithium production properties.

A stock has to meet certain criteria to be considered a penny stock. Such criteria include minimum shareholder equity, market capitalization, and price. If a stock is being traded at a major exchange even if it has a very low price, it isn't considered a penny stock because it is difficult to manipulate the price if it's traded there. In the USA, penny stock transactions are now being regulated by the Securities and Exchange Commission as well as FINRA. In Georgia, its lawmakers drafted and passed a law regarding penny stocks. Other states are now using this law as their template for their own versions. Although there are now restrictions in penny stock trading, these laws are ineffective against pump and dump schemes.

Chapter 4: Finding Your Trading Style

Spread, Market Cap, and Understanding Liquidity

To really capture the main trading styles, you need to understand a core concept to stocks; the bid, ask and spread of a stock. In chapter one I discussed the concept of market capitalization. This simple number represents the total faith that investors and traders have within a company. The larger the market cap, the more assurance you have that a company will continue to prosper, and that even if the stock price tumbles, it will likely be able to recover. The market cap also produces the basic knowledge that you will be able to offload your shares at a later time. This is a paramount aspect to trading penny stocks; regardless of style, you won't be able to make a dime if you cannot offload your holdings. To understand your chances of successfully offloading a stock, you merely have to look at the bid, ask and spread of a stock.

This is a fairly simple concept, but has widespread implications to investing and trading. It can be difficult to see the connection between these metrics and your ability to offload shares, so let me demonstrate this concept using an example. Suppose that you are a stock trader, and you will on holding a stock for just a few hours. You see that the ticker price is $1.87, so you would imagine that it would cost you this amount per share plus brokerage fees to take a position in the stock. In this example, do not worry about the cost of brokers. Even without the added expense from a brokerage firm, the stock is not going to cost you $1.87. This ticker price indicates the last sale of the stock, and how frequently this value updates depends on the exchange. For example, this number might only be updated once every several seconds on the OTCBB, and much sooner on the NYSE.

In this time, the price will have changed by some amount – to account for these rapid changes we have the bid/ask system. This system is essentially a chart with buy and sell orders pegged to prices determined by the traders themselves. For example, suppose that I want to buy this stock for $1.87, my bid price is therefore $1.87. I would put in a buy order with the number of shares that I want and the amount I am willing to pay for it. The sale does not go through until a seller agrees to my bid price.

On the opposite end of this transaction, the sellers have very much the same system. They list the total number of shares that they want to sell, along with an 'ask' price. This ask price is the equivalent of the buyers bid price, and the bid and ask price have to match for a transaction to take place. You can already see that this system is slightly different than just looking at the ticker price and selling for that value or buying for that value. Since there are many traders that likely have the same idea, you end up with this system of bid and ask prices, and transactions only going through when a buyer and seller agree. Think about the implications of this system then – if a stock is quickly picking up in price, the ticker is not that accurate, because the ask prices will be increasing at a greater rate than the bid prices (sellers know that the stock they hold is in demand, and therefore will be asking for more). Conversely, if a stock is on its way down, it would be very hard to sell it for the exact ticker price. There will be many sellers trying to get rid of their stock, and the buyers know this so they will play their bids lower. This means that as a buyer, you typically will buy stock for greater than the stock price when the value is rising, and as seller you will typically sell it for lower than the ticker price if the stock is on its way down.

To encompass the whole system of bid and ask prices, we use something called the 'spread'. The spread is just as essential as the market cap for determining your ability to offload shares. The spread is a function of the difference between the average bid price and the average ask price. If the spread is narrow, meaning the ask and bid prices are close together, we say that a stock is highly liquid. If the spread is wide, meaning the ask and bid prices are far apart, the stock is not very liquid. In short, as a buyer you want wide spreads because this improves your buying ability, and as a seller you want narrow spreads as this means what you are selling is in high demand.

In summary, the market cap and the spread are the pieces of information that we use to determine market liquidity. There are other factors, but at a glance it is these two metrics that will tell you more information than any others. The market cap is useful for determining how difficult it will be to offload your stock in the future (days, weeks and even months). The spread measures your ability to offload shares in the immediate (minutes and hours). Depending on how long you are going to hold onto your assets, you can see how this information plays a vital role in determining your stock picks.

Day Trading:

Day trading is my preferred method of trading. It is this style that I hedge all of my other trading on, meaning that if I don't do well in a few buy and hold investments, I can count on my ability at day trading to make some profit. Day traders have steep time requirements, low capital requirements, and realize their total profits or losses at the end of each trading day. A day trader will spend six to eight hours in front of a computer; identify stocks to buy, and selling them just a few hours later. The market cap requirements for this trading style are the lowest across all styles – you should aim for companies that have a market cap of one million or more dollars.

This strategy revolves around identifying investments through trending data. Trading using this style, a trader does not care what a company offers as material assets. They only care about he stock price, and will be involved for such a short period of time that they do not care about the long term prospects of any one of their investments. A day trader will identify investments by looking at stocks that have had high volatility in the last few days. What a day trader is looking for is predicable volatility, or stocks that has seen shifts of twenty to thirty percent consistently for a few days. Once they can identify the company, and ensure that the market capitalization is more than a million dollars and the spread is narrow (to ensure their ability to offload the stock later), a trader will buy a number of shares in the morning hours of trading. They will repeat this process with four or five other stocks, investing around five percent of their total investment fund in each stock.

The rest of the day for the trader is dedicated to looking for the ideal time to sell stock. The key here is that a trader is using the trending data to find the ideal time to pull out, not necessarily the current ticker price. For example, a trader will have the most favorable spreads to offload stock if they sell before the peak price of a stock has been hit, or even worse if the stock has started to fall in price. To ensure that they sell stock before this happens, a trader will look at the trending data for the last few days. For example, if a stock has a volatility of thirty percent, a trader will start to dump shares around a twenty to twenty-five percent climb in value. Even though the stock price is still going up, it will be so much harder to offload shares when the stock price has peaked that the trader sells before the stock hits this point. Of course, they might sell beforehand if the ticker price indicates a stock in freefall, or the stock does not appear to be matching past trends, but in general the principle is to follow a trend and sell stock before the price peaks or the stock price starts to fall.

Buy and Hold:

You can think about buy and hold trading as simply investing. That is, an investor finds a stock and invests a sizeable portion of their investment fund (up to ten percent) and plans to hold that stock for several weeks or months. An investor finds the ideal company to invest in by looking at the detailed financial reports of the company, and understands the sector of the economy that the company operates in. For example, I have decent knowledge about the market of home lawn maintenance. If I saw a company that was developing a new type of mower, I would maybe have enough knowledge to understand that the mower was a good idea or a bad idea. I would invest depending on if I thought it was a good idea, and the financials of the company were sound. Because so much of this transaction is riding on the detailed financials of a company, I would only make this type of investment if the stock were trading on the NYSE. Remember that the

NYSE has better vetting of the stocks listed than on the OTCBB, making this the ideal exchange for buy and hold trading. This style of trading has the steepest market cap requirements – I would not advise buying into a company with a market cap lower than two million dollars.

Value Trading:

Value trading is the closest thing in investing to a 'sure bet' as there can be, however it requires an extensive amount of research. Investments in value trading are typically on the order of buy and hold trading, that is ten percent of the investment fund, and are investments on the time scale of just a few weeks to few months. For this style of investing, you want to ensure that the market cap of a company is on the order of one and a half to two million dollars. The basic premise to value trading is that you are buying stock in a company that is worth more than the current trading price, and that you can prove it is worth more due to ideas that can be patented, or assets that were never listed on financial reports.

Value trading can be a difficult idea to understand, especially the idea of knowing that a stock is going to go up. The reason that an investor would know that the stock price is going to increase is due to a simple principle about how the price of a stock is determined. Imagine that the stock price of Starbucks went down to one dollar per share. In this event, investors would be running to buy Starbucks. Now you might come to the same conclusion, but almost certainly for different reasons from value traders. The reason that Starbucks is a no brainer purchase at a dollar is that the total number of assets that Starbucks holds is worth far more than their current stock price shows. Starbucks as an intellectual property is worth more than a dollar per share, so is all of the land that Starbucks corporate owns around the world. If we take this example and apply it to penny stocks, we see that most of the unnoticed value in a stock comes from patentable ideas. For example, if you found a compression company on the OTCBB, and discovered that they were about to patent a highly lucrative compression method, this would be a wise investment. You know that the stock price is going to increase because the value of the patentable idea is worth more than the current stock price. In essence, the stock price would have to readjust to the real value of the stock when you factor in the value of the patent. The tricky aspect to this style of trading is that it requires lots of research. In penny stocks, the number of investors that are willing to do this research is comparatively low to larger exchanges, but this lack of competition mostly stems from how difficult it is to find out verifiable information about a company. If you use this method of trading, I suggest that you stick to the NYSE, where financial documents are more likely to be correct, something that you really need to execute the value trading strategy correctly.

Chapter 5: How To Get Started With Penny Stocks

It's time to get your feet wet. This chapter covers everything you need to know to get started trading. As you begin your adventure into trading, be realistic about the amount of time that you can dedicate to research and to monitoring stock quotes. This is a long-term change in your financial future. I want you to start right away, but I want to make sure you have the right mindset. Please refer to Chapter Two for strategies traders use for making a profit and make sure you've had time to digest the information before you make your first trade.

Start Looking At The Exchanges

Penny stocks are traded on three basic exchanges. These range from the extremely reputable NASDAQ to the Pink Sheets, which has no virtually no requirements to have a company listed. The final exchange, and the one you will use the most frequently is the OTCBB, or Over-The-Counter Bulletin Board exchange. This OTCBB has a great selection of penny stocks that meet their minimum standard, but are still appropriately priced at less than one dollar. The NASDAQ does not allow stocks to be listed unless their valued at one dollar or more. Also, the NASDAQ's market capitalization evaluations are more thorough than the other two exchanges, making them a good choice for traders that wish to hold onto stocks for several months at a time.

You will want to look at each and every one of these exchanges. They compete directly with each other and are constantly increasing the services that they offer.

While the Pink Sheets are still not very reputable, they have been trying hard to increase their standing with investors, and the world as a whole. Recently they started the OTCQX – a separate section of the Pink Sheets that offers premium stocks that are more thoroughly vetted. These stocks must meet certain minimums and are broken down into three different categories depending on a stock's value. Familiarize yourself with each exchange, their hours of operation, and perhaps a little bit of their history. The OTCQX has won over a lot of investors and the Pink Sheets is seeing more activity than it has in a long time, but their reputation is still a reason for concern. With their history of improper vetting and low standards, there is little an exchange of that quality can do to change my mind that the stocks they present are evaluated correctly. This does not mean you can't make money on the Pink Sheets – they are in fact a great revenue source for very many investors, but you will want to be aware of their past and know exactly what you are buying and why you are buying it.

After looking at the exchanges and finding your way around the data presented on each, you will want to look at historical data for each exchange to find case histories of given stocks during certain financial conditions. Penny stocks are different than the other exchanges in their minimums, but they still follow the basic rules of economics and shared interaction in financial markets. This means that during rough financial times cosmetic companies, liquor distributors, and makers of small consumable goods do well, when during boom times companies that offer larger scale items do better. Familiarize yourself with some of these trends by looking at a sector that you are interested in. These do not need to be firmly defined sectors, but rather just follow your interests. If you have a fascination for fashion then look at a bundle of clothing companies and see how they have been doing the last few months, or during periods of boom or slowdown in the economy. A lot can be gleamed through this, and you will begin to understand your sector a little bit better with each company that you research. Feel free to look into companies that fall outside of a sector that you have a knowledgebase in, but still keep track of how this industry has been doing recently to give you an idea of general market trends for the future.

Finally, look at how different sectors perform across the different exchanges. You will find that while general market trends are a good predictor of performance of a given sector, exchanges can also dictate the volatility in certain sectors. For example, tech companies listed through he Pink Sheets tend to be much more volatile than tech companies listed on the NASDAQ. This might present itself as a reason to trade on the Pink Sheets, but if you wanted to follow a buy and hold strategy then you would rather buy from the NASDAQ. These stocks will not rise as quickly as what's listed on the

Pink Sheets, but for long term investments they are far more likely to weather the market and have a greater chance of breaking through and getting worldwide recognition. You've read the different types of philosophies of trading and you are probably are aware of which strategy appeals to you. Keep this in mind as you look at the exchanges, taking note of which exchange would work best for your particular strategy and sector of interest.

Start With Zero Investment

After you have looked at the exchanges and familiarized yourself with how they work, you are ready to start investing. Your first step is to pick out several companies and 'buy' stock in quantities that you can afford right now. Do this, but don't actually buy anything. Instead, write down what you want to buy, the number of shares, and the purchase date. You will want to buy shares in quantities that you can actually afford because this is your practice session – you are preparing for real world conditions. For each trade, it's wise to deduct five or ten dollars on the buy and the sell – this mimics the cost of your brokerage's fee. After purchasing stock, sell when you have made a profit, or when the losses have become too great to bare. It can be tempting to cheat in your notebook, write down that you sold at a particular time when you had no intention of selling other than in hindsight. Be truthful to yourself as lying will only do you a disservice.

In addition to keeping track of the stock that you are buying, you will want to record your reasons for purchasing a stock and the number of hours you took to come to your decision. This is a great period for you to look into how many man hours you are putting into investing. This will help you calculate your dollar per hour wage and tell you if you might want to focus on another strategy. Also keep note of your total losses and profits – these numbers are the realistic amount of money that you will make each week.

If you make some really great trades during this practice period, do not be dismayed that you will not actually be receiving any money. Instead focus on what you did right on that trade. There is a set of circumstances on each trade that will lead to profit. Stick to what works for you and you can be consistent. For me, that means swing trading on technology stocks. It's a field that I have some experience in, and while I mostly base my trades on stock price alone, it's nice to know that I can look up a company's background and understand what type of product or service they are selling. I am also aware of existing competitors and the feasibility of success. Find your niche and dig yourself in; you'll want to be in a comfortable place when you first start exchanging money.

Choosing A Broker

Choosing a broker for penny stocks will be a simple process. You just need to determine what broker fits your needs. Brokers differ in their fees, types of service offered, quality of tools available, and minimum buy orders. This is a lot of information, and I'll go over it one by one, but one thing that any broker you choose should have is access to multiple exchanges. Typically with online brokers you can expect access to the NASDAQ and OTCBB. I do not suggest that you trade exclusively on the NASDAQ, but do beware that brokers that specialize in these older exchanges typically have higher rates and larger minimum purchase orders. Right now my go to brokerage firm is LowTraders.com. Note that I will switch if I do find a better brokerage, and you too should be willing to switch if you find better deals.

The most important differentiator between brokers for penny stocks is the fee they require for doing a single trade.

Depending on the amount that you wish to invest, your margins early on might be quite low. You will have to think about deducting a minimum of ten dollars from each trade to cover the buy and sell price for a broker. Five dollars is the lowest I've ever seen, but rates can get much more expensive as you begin to look at fancier services. Brokerage houses that specialize in the Dow Jones and NASDAQ might offer low latency trading, or guarantee that their trades go through faster than anyone else. Don't be fooled, these trades go through at about the same speed regardless of the broker you are using. The difference in time, when there is one, is in the milliseconds. For some traders this is important but it won't be for penny stocks. Plan on using a broker that has a five-dollar transaction free per trade and ignore details of high speed trading.

You will also need to be on the lookout for the type of services offered. Some brokerage firms offer full service and others will simply conduct your trades.

Brokerage firms that have full service clients will be charging more than five dollars per trade, but be aware that they do offer financial advice to their clients, and are generally available for one on one communication. For penny stocks, these types of firms are not particularly useful. Companies that trade at such low values per share are usually not on the radar of firms that offer such services. They might offer to assist you but in practice they will be of little help.

Another differentiator between brokers comes in the tools that they offer. These features are typically the bells and whistles of the brokerage firms. They will offer tools for tracking stocks, sending an email to your inbox when a particular price has been met, and offer much more. It's hard to recommend a brokerage firm based on their set of tools as so many high quality free tools already exist. Depending on your philosophy of trading you might want to splurge if you think a particular tool will be of great help, but a few quick Google searches and you should find something that will work for you just as efficiently. I personally use the OTC market tools. They're a little cumbersome at first, but they aren't so inconvenient that it's worth spending more money for something a little more user friendly.

The last detail you must concern yourself with is the minimum buy order. In addition to any fee on each stock trade, you will also need to buy a minimum number of shares. Some brokerage firms specify an actual number of shares as their minimum, but in the world of penny stocks these minimums are typically the costs of the entire buy order. These will vary between brokers, but you should expect that each trade is at least thirty dollars. While this might seem like an inconvenience, the actual amount you make per share is low enough that you will want to make purchase orders of at least this size. I mentioned it earlier, but currently I use LowTraders.com for most of my purchases. You still will want to look at your other options as new competitors arise all the time. Once you have become ingrained with a particular broker, you will still want to occasionally look at your other options to see if another broker could potentially service you better.

Experiment With Different Philosophies

You should now feel ready to start investing, and hopefully you have gotten enough practice with your journal that you feel welcome to the world of penny stock trading. The approach that you take to trading is a function of your time, your interests, and your capital. You should try a few trades in each approach, regardless of your interest level in any particular method. I suggest this because I have found that people have innate abilities when it comes to investing, and often these abilities differ from what they thought their abilities would be. When I mostly traded on traditional exchanges, I focused on long term trades – it was my niche and I was good at picking winners. I had a strategy of investing in around ten companies and within six months usually one of these paid off well enough to cover my losses on the stocks that didn't do well. I tried this method with penny stocks and it just did not work. I still believe that I am naturally good at long term trades, but that the skill just doesn't translate well to penny stocks. My point here is to keep your mind open and to try other approaches. I never thought that swing trading would be a good fit for me, but now that is virtually the only type of trading I do.

Chapter 6: Tactics And Strategy

In order to have a successful day trading penny stocks market day, you will have to prepare with the info of the day. You have to screen stocks, check on financial news and read trusted forums and message boards. You have to dedicate considerable time to this.

Preparation time is probably the most crucial of your day, as it will determine the stocks you trade and those you do not. By entering the trading day, you have to have your buys and sells planned because you will realize time is gold. I have said it already but you will see it with your own eyes. The idea is for you to make your transactions in a matter of seconds. The idea is that until your experience is well developed, restrict yourself to your pre-watch list and do not pay attention to pop-ups that present to you during trading day. The idea is that you watch the price peaks to sell and not to buy while they keep going up, as this can happen at any moment.

It is important to observe the stocks that have potential to profit because they previously had a high value and in this moment they can be found at ridiculous prices due to some temporary bad news. So it is important for you to get the info on the company's previous development and this way you will have an idea of whether or not the company has enough stability.

When you finish the stock screening and making a stock list that are interesting to you. It is important to analytically check on every stock according to its price and the volume of available shares. It is important to check the values present throughout the last three years.

If you can perceive that the company shows economic stability throughout time, then you have a great candidate. There are a specially good target those shares reaching historical minimal numbers, foreseeing an eventual return. Parting from your daily morning studies, you have to establish a stock top of seemingly interesting shares (from 5 to 10 would be enough. The more stock you follow, less attention you will pay to them). Be aware of eliminating stocks that do not have what you need, as you do not want to make any mistakes.

All this work can take a few hours in the morning, but it is totally fundamental. However, if you want to initiate an investment but have different obstacles that prevent you from dedicating hours to news investigation or even if simply you cannot investigate on this schedule, you can pay for access to a wish list , however, to achieve this you will have to find a provider who adapts to your investment style.

In order to make a fundamental analysis of a stock, you have to define a series of things you will investigate. I will explain in detail the factors that will make a share go up or down in value, besides what I explained earlier about news. Even though many of the companies that list as penny stock have a doubtful reputation and very little published information, this is what will allow you to know if you are taking advantage of a casual inflation or a periodic rise that you can predict (and will allow you to wait for the biggest profit moment, which can be way over your Profit Percentage Gain).

A lot of times you can find patterns in the stock prices of many companies, so having information of their historical progress and legitimacy will help you decide if you should sell when the PPG is reached, in case the contract is not seemed as solid, or keeping those shares because the ascending line can be extended. These conclusions can be achieved only if you get deep access to the info provided by financial sites and your Google searches.

If the chart pattern analysis is your main guide, the fundamental company analysis will make you feel confident in your decision. There is the option of crossing out of the list, given the case the company does not show signs of movement in the share price. However, if the chart analysis indicates that it does, you could have a share to sell in a very short term, in a matter of hours after the trading day has opened. Maintaining a share throughout the day requires that this shows solidity and a possible sustained growth pattern, but this is just a bet.

It is important to critically analyze the news source. The identity and background of the issuing company it is important to consolidate it as valid. And you always have to pay attention and discard the imprecise announcements. An important tip is always checking on the credibility of the two entities that present the agreement, as this will allow to corroborate that both parts are part of the deal.

There are clearly suspicious adds that announce fusions between companies or company acquisitions by consortium and there is no way of detailing the activities of the company. Frequently you find them full of words like "powerful", "target", "high prices during the last years" "next big market move"; these words and phrases frequently appear in scams.

A lot of companies announce their annual earning percentages and sometimes their statements are accessible and through them we can constitute how a 300% annual budget based on revenues turns into a monthly 3% inflated through a small couple of months sample where the earnings reached a drastically peak. Big opportunities are never offered with such an inflated price, so you have to develop a clinical eye to detect prefabricated phrases and holes in crucial information.

The balance sheet of a company tends to be pretty revealing, it shows what you need to know on the economic situation of the company and its proportion regarding what you may find in a press statement. When you look at the balance sheet, you do not want to evaluate the company, you are just checking on in case there are signs that deny the information issued by the company.

Checking the press release can prevent you from getting scammed, as lack of precaution is what makes it possible for others to fool you. Checking if the company has had other press releases on closed businesses is always a good method to understand its earning and expense flow.

A typical scam is presented in the form of an ad showing a company that is "half a million dollars worth" and when you study it you find that its expenses are less than yours.

You got to have a good eye for press releases, because many times I have seen how these are old reposts, which can push you to buy stocks that will not really rise in value. A scam I have seen frequently is the one of companies with a doubtful location; it is important they offer details regarding their address, as many countries have laws that allow these scams to happen with impunity.

Try to do a research on the information regarding employees and company directives, this can reveal extremely important information. It is hard to believe that a company with less than 10 unrelated employees who do not have any relationship with the industry related to the company.

Chapter 7: Managing Risk And Understanding Your Profitability

A Basic Rule to Follow

Most trades that you partake in will be about five percent of your total investment fund. This is done to ensure that you never deplete your investment fund in a few trades, and that you live long enough in investing that you can make a profit. The absolute maximum that you want to invest in a stock is ten percent of your investment fund. This is a very simple rule, but is one that is very hard to stay committed to, especially when you are just starting off. For the beginner investor, I suggest that you start your investment fund with around $2000, with an absolute bare minimum of $1000. Anything less and you will be exposing yourself to too much risk per any one trade.

For example, suppose that your starting investment fund is $2000. From this amount, you know that your average trade should be around $100. The amount of profit that you can expect to make from a single day trade with $100 isn't that much, about $16-$20 depending on the brokerage fee and the swing of the stock. This is why there is such a temptation to invest $300 or more in a single stock, but the truth is that early on you will be making just a few more investments that pay off than in which you lose. You will lose on some investments; this is must a matter of fact. If you only make $16 on a single trade, this might seem like you are hindering yourself, but it also means that you can expect maximum losses of only $16-$30, at the very most. No one trade is going to make you very rich, but that's not the point. The point is that no one trade will wipe you out either.

For larger investments, on the order of a buy and hold strategy, you will want to bet closer to around ten percent of your investment fund. This is the maximum that you should be investing however, so you see that you need quite a large investment fund to make money from these other styles of trading. I wouldn't partake in a buy and hold or value trading strategy for any less than $1000 for example, meaning that your investment fund needs to be somewhere between ten and twenty thousand dollars.

You will likely start with day trading, earning very small and modest profits in the beginning, however this is always proportional to your investment fund. If you are starting off with $2000, then you might only make one hundred to two hundred dollars of profit each week, but as your investment fund grows, this number grows as well. With a 100k investment fund for example, you can expect to make five to ten thousand dollars per week with some successful trades. Just remember the ten percent rule, and your ability to make a profit is always proportional to your investment fund, and you will need to beef up that investment fund before you can start making large sums of money every week in trading.

Diversification

Understanding the ten percent rule allows you to diversify your investments. Essentially, once you begin to follow the ten percent rule, you immediately will start to diversify your investments. The one caveat to diversification is to not invest purely for the sake of investing, or at least early on. What I mean is that you do not need to make four or five trades everyday for day trading when you are just starting out. You should only make this number of trades if you feel comfortable with all of the stocks that you are buying. If you feel less than comfortable on two or three of these investments, then you simply should not make them. It is likely that you will spend and receive your entire investment fund back in a single week (it's only twenty investments and you make the profit/loss each day), but if you cannot hit this target, you should not try. As long as you stick to your guns about the ten percent rule, then you will find the investment opportunities for you are such that you are naturally diversifying your investments.

Once you reach a point of having an investment fund above ten thousand dollars, you may want to start getting into other types of trading, namely buy and hold and value trading. While value trading takes a lot of time and research to execute correctly, buy and hold trading is much more specific to the knowledge that you have about a sector of the economy. This is the second tier of diversifying your investments. You may focus on day trading as your primary strategy but in the background have one or two buy and hold investments. The important concept here is that you are hedging your bets with the buy and hold trading by investing most of your money in something that you are already capable of succeeding in; in this case, day trading. Make your primary way of making profit your most reliable method of trading, followed by slightly diversifying and trying a secondary method. Your secondary method is the risky bet, while your primary method is the safer. For example, as I transitioned into penny stocks I started with a fairly large investment fund from savings. I actually truly started in this business as a value trader, and would hedge my day trading based on the value trades that I did. For each investor this will be different but the idea is always the same – ensure your more risky investments by doubling down on the style of investing that you are more confident in.

Understanding Your Investment Fund

You have a good idea of the different styles of investing in penny stocks, and you understand that each of these styles have different capital requirements. In order from largest to smallest pools of capital needed, you have: buy and hold, value trading and day trading. I highly suggest that everyone starts off with day trading, just because the investment to start with will be the smallest of any trading style. It also allows starting traders to get used to interacting with the different tools for analysis on their preferred brokerage firm's website. Lastly and most important, day trading allows for a trader to reap the profits from trading very quickly. This allows you to build up your investment pool and increase the amount that you can make per trade. All of this plays into the ten percent rule of investing, and early on you should be trying to expand the amount of money that you have to invest.

There are a few notes that must be mentioned about investing funds. This advice comes from the mistakes that I have seen other rookie traders make, so while it may seem obvious to not make some of these mistakes, I've seen them repeated plenty of times before. There are three essential rules that you must follow with your investment fund: one, the money that you are using for trading is money that is only used for trading. Two, the profits that you reap may be used to inflate your investment fund, but never invest one hundred percent of your proceeds into your capital fund. Three, accurate record keeping makes or breaks investors.

The first rule might seem to be the most simple, but this is where I've seen most new investors falter. Your investment fund needs to be wholly separate from all of your other accounts. That means that the money that you use for rent, college, savings and retirement need to be wholly separate from your investment fund. No matter the temptation, do not inflate your investment fund with money that you have saved for other purposes. There are some obvious reasons why you want to do this, but the most important is that this gives you greater freedom in your investments. This not so obvious reason allows you to be more committed to the investments that you do make. Knowing that the money that you are betting with is money specifically set aside for investing allows you to make wiser decisions in your investments, and stick to your convictions.

The second rule is that you have to pay yourself out of your profits, not out of your investment fund. You might invest some portion of your profits back into your investment pool, increasing the maximum size of any single investment that you make, but don't put one hundred percent of your profits back into your investment fund. The reason for this is that the separation of accounts is extremely important to ensuring a long and fruitful trading career. If you invest all of your profit in your investment fund, it muddies the mind, creating an inclination that the money in your investment fund can be used for something other than investing. The moment you take money out of your investment fund to use for anything other than stock investments, you have created the first step to depleting your investment fund and losing your profits. Make sure you separate your profits, and only draw from your profit fund for life's necessities. This mostly ties into the first rule, but is used to greater ensure that your investment fund stays separate from everything else in your life.

The third rule is to keep an accurate log of all of your trades. I have seen many traders make a profit at the end of the week, but they aren't entirely clear about where that profit came from. They can give me the rough percentages of where that profit came from, meaning from what picks, but they have a hard time articulating exactly what they did right and what they did wrong. Your success as a trader is entirely dependent on your ability to improve. To improve, you need to keep an accurate log of all of your trades, writing the exact amount that you made or lost on any single investment. The more information you include in your trade log, the better. The most useful piece of information that you can include is your reasons for why you made a particular investment. You need to write exactly why you made a purchase, whether it was based on trending data or any other strategy. From here, you can determine your strengths and weaknesses as a trader, and focus on the style that earns you the most profit.

Chapter 8: The Habit Of Managing Your Emotions At All Times.

This habit is connected to habit number three. When you use your extra money in your investment, you avoid the pitfalls of a roller coaster emotional ride. There is no strong attachment to the money, therefore, there is less possibility of depression when you lose the money or over elation when you gain more money. You would want to be as much as "unemotional" as you can when it comes to stock trading. This will pave the way for logic to work rather than emotions. The more unattached you are to the money, the better you can manage your stock trading.

Stock trading can affect your emotions as much as love can if you would let it. This comes as no surprise as we know that your heart follows your treasures and vice versa, your treasures follow your heart.

Money is a form of treasure by most people. And that is an acceptable notion, what with all the energy, effort and time we give to acquire more money. So it hurts to lose some thing, which is precious for a person. A lot of people committed the error of putting all their money in one investment and when that particular trade collapsed, all their money came down with it. Many became hysterical and depressed. It was not just about money anymore. It was about their future, their means of survival, their everything. And then they have nothing in one day. All of their hard work went to the drain.

The thing with losing is it makes you desperate and foolish. You try to regain everything by investing some more. The wise move of admitting your mistake, cutting the loss, learning from that mistake and starting over again seem inappropriate during the height of desperation. Stop. When you suffer a great loss, the next best thing to do is to pause. Do not be moved by fear that you need to reinvest and win back the losses. This could cause more losses.

Losing money in stock trading is expected. But being emotional about the loss can be avoided. The strategy of using extra money you can afford to lose would make you "unemotional" when it comes to losses. Becoming unattached to the money you invest in stocks is important in keeping a clear head. Only invest the extra money that you can afford to let go. Do not ever, ever invest everything, your all in all. You could do that but it will keep you on the verge of insanity all the time. That is suicide. Remember, just your extra money. Period.

Emotions can be positive or negative. You should not also be "emotional" with gains. The thing with winning is it sometimes makes you greedy. You want more. The number one error of new stock traders is to be excited with a gain and invest more and more to that particular trade or other stocks without considering all sides. A gain or a win now is not a guarantee of a win or gain tomorrow. Actually, history and statistics would show that a downfall or a crash usually occurs after a gain. So be careful in putting more and more money just because you were emotionally excited by the winnings. Again, keep a calm attitude and clear your minds of any emotions before you decide on your next move for investing.

Having a clear head therefore, whether you have a gain or loss, is vital. So in good or bad times, be emotionally neutral. Avoid being reckless with your stock trading. As mentioned earlier, it is so unpredictable. Staying emotional stable is vital in becoming a success in stock trading.

Chapter 9: Understanding The Psychology Of Trading And How It Affects You

Many stock traders would like to bear the title The Penny Stock Prophet but in reality most just do not have what it takes.

Predicting the behaviour of Stocks and of the market has been aspired to since the stock markets were established.

Penny stocks are stocks traded under $5 on smaller exchanges and are sometimes referred to as micro cap investments. Do not be fooled by the small price of the stocks as enormous gains and huge losses are possible in this volatile arena.

One of the reasons it is so difficult to predict small stocks is the lack of reliable information or even manipulated information distributed by the companies representing the shares. Many company shares traded for pennies have been previously declined or removed from a major stock exchange such as NASDAQ. Sometimes this is due to lack of consistent and reliable reporting of company activity.

Veteran investors know where to turn for information on current shares and have additional tools to cross check an analyse the performance of trades over time. Experienced traders also have the accumulated understanding of how the stock markets behave.

Information and calculations on share prices, company movements and expected gains most often do not comprise the entire equation for picking penny stocks to invest. A true Penny Stock Prophet will also have a proven algorithm to assist in his decision making.

A variety of trading tools are commercially available. You may also find free information spread judiciously across the Internet. When selecting your information source it is important to verify that the website does not have a conflict of interest with the recommended stocks. such disclosure is required by law, but may not be easily found.

One of the variables associated with stock trading is the main force driving stock share prices, also referred to as Psychological Support Level (PSL). This variable helps identify undervalued stocks.

PSL is similar to formulas currently used by mathematicians to predict and determine how human behavior affects population growth, crime and even terrorism called Psychometric Science.

Pros and Cons

When an investor has a particular set of penny stocks to watch, it is often described as an exceptional sense of penny stock trading because such investor already has a focus and may not likely be a victim of the mistakes of others. Having a personal penny stocks to watch list can be a bit challenging because of the fact that there are two sides to it in terms of advantages and disadvantages. It is only a pity today that just few people actually understand that being too focused at times can lead to blind dogmatism which may eventually results in missing vital opportunities in the market.

One major characteristic of a successful stock trader is dynamism. This implies you have to show certain element of creativity in your treading adventures and that there are circumstances you have to solely depend on your full discretion in order to make an impression. Regrettably, this may not be an attribute of a loyal fan of penny stocks to watch because you are possibly not going to realize the need to try something different and explore other opportunities once you have made up your mind for penny stocks to watch. What I mean in essence is that one of the disadvantages of the penny stocks to watch trading method is your inability to exercise your creativity since you now feel relaxed with a particular group of stocks.

Another major challenge with this method is the fact that investors now seem to be psychologically tied to their investments in those stocks and as a result may not readily be sensitive to vital chameleon market changes. And since being sensitive to the chameleon changes in the market as an investor gives an edge over others, you really need not to be over dependent on penny stocks to watch in the first place, not to talk of losing your creative instincts to optimize these opportunities. The lack of originative instincts in stock traders can also be said to be responsible for majority of losses apart from other inevitable individual lapses.

The sense in this writing is not to scare you from being a fan of penny stocks to watch, is only meant to teach you how you can make the best out of this viable stock trading techniques. In fact, the advantages are so enormous when juxtaposed with the highly heralded disadvantages. In actual sense, you would be a better trader and a winner that is able to defy every rumor with a unique sense of humor because you already have a focus.

Chapter 10: Techniques For Making Money With Penny Stocks

Because of their cheap prices and affordability, many beginners like to invest in penny stocks. Critics of this breed of stocks however raise a red flag that investing in penny stocks is one of the riskiest behavior that a beginner investor can take in the entire stock market. Even though the share prices of these stocks are often low, the dollar values of these stocks are accompanied by more volatility and huge risks. The paradox is that Financial Times and other financial media reports indicate that penny stocks have gained popularity over the recent past and many people are harvesting big in this trade.

In this chapter, we analyze in great depth some of the techniques, strategies and steps that you will undertake to invest reasonably and prudently to start making money in the penny stock market.

At a more basic level, you should never forget to do your homework

If you decide to walk down this road, then you cannot ignore your role. Like any other trade the most basic part of your homework is to find out information about the investment decision you are about to undertake.

Your homework should encompass the following:

Knowing The Factors That Make Penny Stocks Risky

Several factors come into play when it comes to discussing the risky nature of penny stocks. We had discussed this before in this book and we really do not need a repetition. These factors include insufficient information about the penny stock market, lack of regulation in the sector especially for the OTC stocks and the illiquid nature of these stocks. Therefore, it is important that you understand the risk in the sector before deciding to swim in this sea keeping in mind that investing is about keeping the risk at its possible minimum while maximizing returns at its greatest maximum.

Opening A Brokerage Account

This is no child play. You need an easy way to transact and this is where a brokerage account becomes more than a necessity. Technology has made this very simple and you can sign up for an online brokerage account that charges minimal annual fees and low commissions at the comfort of your couch.

Your brokerage account should give you the information that you need to make sound financial decisions. These should include charts, graphs, historic data and any other relevant piece of information that can assist you make a good pick.

Checking Trade Status For Penny Stocks

Perhaps the best starting point would be to ask why penny stock is trading lowest. Financial experts argue that there is always a reason behind any low price. Try as much as you can to buy shares that are trading through a regular exchange. Even though penny stocks also trade on OTC, this comes with additional risk.

Secondly, always check on listing status of already established penny stocks. You realize that some already established penny stocks may fall in value so much that it is almost tempting to invest in such stocks with hopes that they will jump up. If a company is perilously moving closer to bankruptcy, then this can be investment suicide. If a company reaches a point to which it is delisted, then there is reason for investing in such stocks and there would be a warning sign for you on the penny stock ticker.

Do Not Believe In Hypes

One way with which fraudsters net their victims is using pump and dump schemes. Additionally, should you come across emails recommending a particular stock, first check the disclaimers. If the promoter is being paid for the advert, steer away from that stock. Good undervalued stocks are often kept secret not advertised in public media.

Do not let the allure of quick cash ruin your investment journey. There are much better ways of making money with penny stocks.

Choosing Your Strategy

Warren Buffet believes that doubling your investments is a realistic dream that every investor should strive for. He, however, says that this is only possible if an investor develops sound strategies before committing their funds. You may not own the same shares as warren buffet but the rule is clear. You must have a strategy- a sound one for this matter. Consider employing the following strategies in your portfolio:

Sell Quickly Strategy

I always advise investors not to fall in love with penny stocks. Some people become too attached to their stocks to the extent that they want to hold them for eternity. Do not be so greedy as to wait for a 1000% return. Once you have achieved a certain satisfactory level of profit, consider selling the stock, and repeat the investment cycle. This strategy will prevent you from losing a bird that is already in your hands while chasing for two in the bush. The penny stock market is very volatile and full of uncertainties and you cannot risk holding the stocks for an unnecessary long time.

Buy And Hold Strategy

This is where investors buy cheaper stocks and hold them until such a time that the penny stock experiences a significant price increment. While buy and hold strategy may somehow be a good bet for other ordinary stocks, for penny stocks it might turn to a bad proposition. When it works, you can be sure to be rich overnight. However, with the volatile penny stock market, you may lose big with this strategy. So this strategy is never a win-win strategy and therefore you need tread carefully.

Diversify Your Stock

Consider making a portfolio of penny stocks drawn from different companies. Experts think that it is in penny stocks that portfolio diversification produces the best results. This is because most of these companies have problems that are only specific to them. So if the stock of company B performs below your expectations, this can be compensated with the good performance of penny stock D.

The bottom line is that you need a strategy and you cannot just start trading without a winning strategy. Depending on your circumstances, you can go for a sell quick or buy hold strategy. The secret is that each strategy suits each stock and one that works for A may not necessarily work for B. Do your homework well then.

Opting For High Volume Stocks

Penny stocks are generally not liquid. As a beginner, the liquidity of your stocks is so necessary to be compromised. You need to have a stock that you buy and sell easily. That is why, you need stocks that trade at least 100000 shares each day. This kind of penny stocks is the safest bet for you. Penny stocks that trade at low volumes can give be a nightmare to sell.

Not Overtrading

The allure of buying large and making big money can be so much overwhelming. Trading over 10% of the stock's volume can look appealing but this may be very detrimental to your investment portfolio. This is because it is very difficult to unload such a big volume of stock.

The above are obvious things that any prudent penny stock investor cannot afford to ignore. They are general that many beginners fail to observe and end up furthering the perception that penny stocks is an investment for investors who want to lose their pennies. This is a fallacy and you can overcome it by starting with the most obvious rules.

Chapter 11: How Penny Stocks Prices Vary

As we saw in the previous chapter, there are stocks that are priced really low and traded on a regular basis in the stock market. These stocks are mostly influenced by several internal and external factors that cause its value to rise up and drop down on a daily basis. Penny stocks are slightly more predictable as their market is much different from regular stock markets. So it is easier for you to trade in penny stocks as compared to normal stocks. However, it is important to understand the various factors that influence penny stocks and how their prices vary.

The prices of penny stocks are usually influenced by their demand and supply as well as the specific assets or earnings of the particular company. This means that where there is a high demand and the supply is low, the prices will increase. This is usually the best time to sell the stocks and earn your huge margins. Since we rely on demand and supply to make profits from trading in penny stocks, you may not necessary evaluate the market but rather what could increase or decrease the prices so that you can know the best time to buy and the best time to sell.

Similarly, have an eye out on the news, as there will be stories available about the particular company. These stories will tell you whether or not the stock of a company will do well. Generally, any changes in the company's board members or an announcement of their profits will cause the price of the share to surge. Similarly, if there is a loss reported, then the price will plummet. You have to understand this trend and establish a pattern where you first check the news and then decide on a stock to buy, or stay away from. Let us look at it in detail.

The Fourth Estate And Penny Stocks

Typically, the media plays a key role in providing a catalyst in the price shift of penny stocks. Negative news of a certain company may cause their stocks to go down while positive news may make them go up. This is not always the case so a closer look and analysis is required before making your prediction. The trick is to determine whether the news is good enough to increase the price of instructions.

You can subscribe to a news journal that sends you alerts every now and then. Reading regularly is extremely important. There is no point in reading today and forgetting about it tomorrow. You must pay keen attention to the companies that issue penny stocks. Ensure that you know how to interpret the news. There can be several interpretations of the same news and you must understand it correctly, otherwise, you won't make the right choice for yourself. You must also personally go through the company's balance sheet if you want to understand it from the different points of view.

You can also watch the news and look at all the updates. They will provide you with all the best picks and help you understand which stock is a better choice for you.

Below are some sections of news to look out for as a beginner or potential investor in penny stocks to help you out

Insider Buying

If employees of a given company begin to buy shares of their own company, it is a sign that something good is coming up and so it is good to invest in shares of that company.

Reverse Mergers

This is just money in the bank. Some companies in the penny stock market are there to serve no major purpose except to function as a way for private companies to go public. This results in transfer of ownership from private individuals to the public. The private company normally has assets generates revenue but with a reverse merger, a former non-functional company suddenly acquires new assets and revenues. This is reflected by the price of stocks.

Survival From Bankruptcy

When a company announces it could be going bankrupt, their stock prices go down suddenly. Later, the company might announce that it has made a detailed plan of escaping bankruptcy and this might cause the prices of its sock to go up. This is a good chance for an investor to buy the stocks when the prices are at an all time low and then gain in value when they go up again. Some companies though can use this technique to influence the prices of their stocks.

New Patent

A right to a new patent by a penny stock company is good news in that, it shows that in future there will be high revenue numbers.

Affiliation With A Big Company

Many people will want to be associated with big shots. If a re-known company is planning to do business with a penny stock company, then that is a clear indication of the future potential growth of that company. Big companies choose their business partners carefully. That means it is advisable to invest in that company.

Quarterly Financial Numbers

Great quarterly numbers bring about a sudden increase of prices to reflect the current quarterly numbers of the company. This can be due to various causes such as an increase in the number of contracts, royalty fees, and higher demand for products or services.

Positive Signs to Look for

As you know, prediction is everything when it comes to penny stock buying. You need to understand whether or not the price of the stock will rise soon or if it will drop down. More than the latter, it is the former that you need to consider carefully if you wish to make the most of your penny stocks.

Here are some signs that will tell you if your penny stocks are on the verge of rising up.

Money movement

The very first thing to look at is whether or not any money is moving into or out of the share. This will have a big impact on the price fluctuations of the share. If the company has introduced newer shares or split the old ones then that is also of relative significance. You can check the movement of money using the technical analysis and see whether any fresh money has been pumped into the shares. Check the on balance volume and see if it is on the upper side. If it is, then the price of the share will start to move upwards any time and you must be prepared to buy the stocks, as its share value will surge up. On the contrary, if the on balance volume is low, then the price per share will plummet. So that is indication for you to get rid of the stock as soon as possible lest you be stuck with stocks that will not fare well in the near future.

Trading volumes

The next thing to look for in a stock is the trading volume. You must look at the number of stocks being bought and sold. If there is a surge in the number of buyers then rest assured, the price of the stock will rise. You must also look at the ratio between the buyers and the sellers to have a clear idea of where the price of the stock will head. If there are many buyers and few sellers then the stock price will surely rise. But if there are lesser buyers and many sellers then the stock prices will go down. If there is a sudden movement in the volumes then you must prepare to take appropriate action. Here, there must be a double spike in the trading volumes, which will tell you whether or not it is important to note the change.

Precedence

Looking at past records is the best way to tell whether the price of a stock will rise. So look at what the company's management did in the past to understand whether your stock's price will raise or fall. The company's CEO and top management members make this decision. By checking the past records, you can see if the company has taken any action on the shares and its values. Many companies will decide to split the share and announce bonus shares, this will cause people to buy more, as the company's shares will half and turn affordable. It will subsequently cause a spike in the share's price. This is a great opportunity for you to capitalize upon and buy the shares and then sell it again when its prices have high.

News

Any company that manages to remain in the news for a long time is sure to benefit in the stock market. It is a lot like advertising. When you watch an advertisement, you will feel like buying the product. Similarly, you will feel like buying stocks of a company whose good news is doing the rounds. The news can be in regard to its fundamentals or its technical or something to do with its products. All of this will cause it to remain in the news and you can benefit from it. Just make sure you tune into the news and also hear about companies from your social circles. If there is good news then the price will definitely rise up in the near future and if there is bad news, then the price will fall for sure.

Market capture

When a company increases its market share, it is clear indication that its products are doing well in the market. You will definitely benefit from the company's stocks and must buy them at the earliest. It will also mean an increased pressure on the competitors and that will cause their shares to be affected as well. So you must check whether you have shares of their company and decide whether to hold or sell them before it gets affected further.

Results

As soon as a company announces results, there will surely be a change in its share price. If the results are good then obviously there will be a rise in the price and if the results are bad then there will be a drop in the price per share. You must be aware of when the results of the company will be announced and whether it is best for you to buy, hold or sell the stock.

Small vs big

You must understand that a large company's small shares are always better than a small company's large shares. So, look for a multi million companies whose shares are quite less in the market as opposed to a small company whose shares are more. Although contrarians will pick the latter, it is up to you to choose the type that will fit your investment need the best. With the former, it will be easier to predict the impact of market trends as opposed to the latter. So you will have something that is easy to foretell and not be stuck with shares that are not following any trend.

High low patterns

There is general belief in the stock market that a stock that has been dipping will continue to dip and a stock on the rise will continue to raise. However, the contrarian belief says a stock on the rise will dip and a dipping stock will rise. Both of these are valid views but you must look for the highest highs and the highest lows in a stock. If a stock ends up dipping below its 1 year low then the stock is in trouble, and not going to move upwards any time soon. Similarly, if the stock has hit a high much higher than its 1 year high then it is a great stock to invest in and it is best that you choose that stock for yourself.

Chapter 12: Trading Penny Stocks

We have given you some really appropriate tools and information so far in this book that will lead you to your daily or weekly trading routine. Buying penny stocks is great, but they will do you no good monetarily if you don't trade them and maximize your return on investment. Trading is just as strategic as picking the stocks that you want to purchase and it all kind of melds together into a fluid process where you are trading and buying like a machine. The penny stock industry is definitely something you will have to pay close attention to and though you may not be able to be online all of the time, it is important to check your stocks several times a day and set up alerts that will assist you in catching stocks at their maximum potential for return. Investing in your future is usually something you do while also going about your normal life with work, family, and routine so adding some time in for your trades will be essential for success.

We are not going to get into giving you a step by step process of how to physically sell your stocks. Between the brokerage service you have chosen and the tips and information we have given so far, the technical process should come relatively quickly to you. What does need some attention are the things that you need to remember when you are going through the process of trading. In this chapter, we are going to dive into the best practices for trading your penny stocks. Some of the information may seem repetitive, but that means it is a vital part of the entire process and should be remembered at each turn in your investment strategy. From reading your stocks to selling your shares at the precise moment for maximum returns, let's take a look at the ten most important best practices to successful penny stock management and trading.

One-Success Stories

No matter where you look when you Google penny stocks you are going to find a million stories of success where people turned a thousand dollars into a million dollars. Some of these stories will be articles while others will be those ridiculous schemes asking you to buy their book or hire them to show you how to do the same. No matter what the angle of the success story, ignore it. Don't sign up for extra info, don't be impressed by shiny numbers and short time periods, and don't believe everything you see; this guy may have five students who reached a million dollars in three years but what he doesn't tell you is he has seven hundred thousand students.

Like so many other things in life, there is no magical formula to get you from rags to riches in thirty days. The best thing for you to do is to put your nose to the grind, follow the rules, use your best practices, and focus on your goals. It feels superb when selling your first stock for a positive return but don't run away with that feeling. Instead, use it to see what you did right and wrong and tweak your practice so that the next intelligent purchase you make will yield even higher returns on investment. This investment is for you and your specific goals and if one of them is to make a million dollars you might want to ensure your portfolio is highly diversified because you are not going to find that quick million in penny stocks.

Two-Tips and Disclaimers

When you start buying and selling penny stocks, you are going to find newsletters and emails popping up all over the place. Do not be fooled by the "tips" in these publications; no one gives the info up for free. The SEC requires a company to put a disclosure at the end of an article or promotion if they are being compensated in any way by the parent company of the stock they are promoting. Make sure to check all of the promotions for that disclosure and ignore that information; it's no different than buying shoes from a chain store because the ad says they are the best.

A lot of times you will see stocks reach their 52-week peak, not because the company is doing so well, but because several publications picked up the ad the company paid to place. These tips are useless and can lead you to purchase stock that will crash shortly thereafter and yield you little to negative return on investment. As with anything else, do your research about a company before you purchase and trade. Always ignore the publicized tips and disclaimers about buying specific stock.

Three-Speed Of Sale

One of the biggest mistakes you can make is expecting a thousand percent return on a penny stock. If you wait for that kind of performance, I can promise you will lose more money than you make. A safe and healthy return on a stock is twenty to thirty percent within a few days. This level of return is what makes penny stocks so popular in the investment arena, a relatively stable return in a really short amount of time. Ultimately you are buying in bulk and selling quickly so you may only be making pennies to small dollars on each stock, you are doing that in bulk, in a quick time period, and with little to no work.

This quick turn around on penny stocks is what enables you to make a substantial weekly return on investment because the turnaround time for profit is so short. However, watch out for that devil on your shoulder whispering to stay just a little longer because even if you notice later that stock continued to climb, you saved yourself in the long run because most will top out on returns at that thirty percent mark. Penny stocks are already high risk, don't add to that risk with your behavior in trading.

Four-Company Management

The companies offering the stock will often have many different, but all outstanding, things to say about their business and its future. Just like the promotions you can not believe anything these management members have to say. Would you buy a car from the guy who owns the car company just because he says it's the best car on the market? No, probably not. These companies will say and do anything they can to get you to purchase their stock, and some of the companies are not actually real companies. Many people will create a "company," sell stock and reap the rewards of the return on a company that only exists on paper.

One of the most important points that you need to remember is that no matter what line of stocks you are trading, there are always people trying to rip you off. With penny stocks, the stakes are higher because the regulations are lower when it comes to what is expected through the SEC. Don't believe something until you have gotten the information from a reputable source. If it seems to good to be true, it probably is. Do your research, understand the company, and if in doubt either pass on the stock or go to a professional who will be able to lead you better in the direction you should follow.

Five-Short Selling

A short sale is kind of an opposite way of thinking about stocks. When you purchase a stock, you are hoping its value will rise so that you can sell that stock and make a profit. For example, you buy one share of X Company stock at $100 and the next week the share is worth $150; you could technically sell that stock and make a fifty percent return on investment. Short selling is when an investor borrows a stock has it sold and then hopes the price on the stock goes down so that they can buy it back and make the profit.

For example; Joe borrows ten shares worth $50 and sells them. The 500 dollars is put into his account, and he waits. If the stock goes up to $75 within a week, he will have to buy the shares back, but he will lose money. If the shares go down to $25 he has to buy the shares but he will have made a fifty percent return. There are a lot of rules on the process, but it must go through a broker.

Due to the volatility of penny stocks, it is never a good idea to short sell them. Though some of them might be appealing, you never know if they have been pumped up due to promotion. These two factors make it hazardous to short sell penny stock and the outcomes very rarely outweigh the risk.

Six-Volume

Depending on the brokerage firm, Penny stocks are defined as stocks between less than a dollar and five dollars a share. Due to their low cost you want to buy these stocks in volume in order to maximize your return on investment. Trading penny stocks would be pointless if you were trading one share at a time, making.30 a trade. You are trying to maximize your return and do it within a certain timeframe that you set out when planning your goals and financial assessments. However, be reasonable because if you purchase ten thousand dollars worth on one stock and it plummets you have just lost a lot of money. Find a happy medium between too little and too much when purchasing shares of penny stocks.

When it comes to the volume, you also want to focus that into what stocks you are buying. You want to stay with companies that are selling at least 100,000 shares of stock a day. If you choose stocks with the lower trading volume, you may find yourself in a position where you have a hard time selling that stock off later. If a company's stock has less than 100,000 trades a day and isn't worth more than fifty cents you probably want to leave it alone and move on to something else.

Seven-Stops

Stops were discussed in the last chapter, but there are two ways to look at stops. Most people would say it is smart to utilize your brokerage sites stop loss tool in order to keep yourself from plummeting too far into the negative when a stock doesn't do well. If you are not a person steadily watching the market then you will want to use the stop loss on every purchase you make. However, there is another way to handle this that is slightly riskier and requires self-control and self-interest.

Mental stops are just that; setting your stops based on what you think is best with the stock. You will look at the share and decide what you want to get out of it and then make a mental note of where the cut-off point is. This tactic takes skill and practice in the market, and though risky, can lead to higher rates of return. Mostly you are pushing the boundaries of your stock with no fallback, but your ability to start and stop where you think is best.

Eight-The Best

Without a doubt, you always want to strive to buy the best stock on the market at that given point in time. One of the ways is to track a stock and buy the highest one at its fifty-two-week mark, especially if the stock has seen overall growth. Sometimes this process will take some time, and you will have to track a particular stock for weeks before purchasing it. This dedication is the same as taking the time to research a company before buying its stock. You want to be sure of your investments and treat each and every one as if it is the diamond in the rough that will lead you closer to your goals.

It can be difficult sometimes to watch a stock climb and jump but start to decline when you are ready to purchase, but this is part of the game. You can't always predict what a stock will do, in fact, you can rarely predict what one will do. Sometimes a stock may be doing amazing, but you wake up, and the CEO has passed away with no heir to his thrown, and down the stock prices go. Research and patience, however, can pay off in the long run.

Nine-Large Portions

This essential practice is crucial and is often overlooked. When you purchase penny stocks you are buying in volume but when you sell you don't want to do the same. First of all, you want to limit your stock size regardless of its promise so that you are always able to get out of stock quickly if it begins to decline. When you go to sell the stock, though, regardless of its status you want to space out what you are selling. A good rule of thumb is to never sell more than ten to fifteen percent of the stock's daily volume.

For example, if you bought ten thousand shares of a stock and it is time to sell, you don't want to sell all ten thousand shares at one time. If the daily volume is five thousand, then you want only to sell 500-750 shares of stock a day until it is gone. Of course, if there is an emergency you can sell all of the stock at once but it is safer to sell it in batches then to make significant share sales at once. Some investors may see the large sale as a sign that the stock is not doing well or predicted to do poorly in the upcoming days, making it hard to sell.

Ten-Keep It Professional

Always remember that there is a reason that penny stocks have earned a bad reputation regardless of how well you do at them. Every company will tell you that they have revolutionized the business, that their products will explode, and there aren't any other companies like them in the world. Regardless of your research always stay cynical and careful with your stock purchases. Don't fall in love with a company or a stock even if they stand for everything you do; it is not a smart choice.

You will also find that when you talk to friends and family about your entrance into the penny stock arena, everyone will have an opinion and a suggestion. Though they may be trying to help, make your own choices through solid research and following the guidelines you have set up for yourself. Diversity is incredibly important not just for your overall portfolio but for you penny stock portfolio as well. Stay smart and do what is best for you and your goal tracks and try not to listen to other people and their suggestions.

It is entirely possible to make excellent rates on returns, but you have to be knowledgeable, understand the game, and always have an eye open for scammers who tend to run the penny stock trade. Some investors do not have the kind of capital to purchase shares of Google, so penny stocks are perfect for them. If a stock choice works out then, that person could see huge profits. If you buy a thousand shares of thirty cent stock and that stock goes up to a dollar, you just made four thousand dollars. However, to be smart, you would sell that stock when it reached fifty to seventy-five cents and roll with that return on investment. Yes, you want to maximize your investments, but you want to do it in a safe manner and not hedge bets on companies that may or may not be there when you wake up in the morning. Waiting for a stock to quadruple in the penny stock arena is risky and rarely happens so capitalize on your gains and move forward.

This chapter has given you the ins and outs of the best practices to follow when trading your stocks. These are just initial practices and as time goes on you will be able to add to your list of do's and dont's that work for you with penny stocks. The common theme in penny stock trading is using your head and researching everything. You also must always be aware that there are people and companies out there looking to cheat you out of your investments which can ultimately set you back in your goals. Now that you have the understanding of how to purchase and trade your penny stocks you will need to know how to track them in the system so that you can make a right decision on when to sell. Tracking your assets can be difficult, but due to the popularity of stocks, most companies have created excellent systems to track different stocks and all at the touch of your fingers.

Chapter 13: General Trends In Stock Trading

General trends to analyze:

Now that you have calculated the internal factors, let's see what external factors dictate market trends:

- Social Trends
- Political Trends
- Consumer trends
- Industrial situation
- Economic conditions
- Policies of the governments
- Global political situation

Social Trends:

Trading on penny stocks is hugely dependent on the social trends of the product the company is selling. A small startup could accelerate extremely rapidly if their products hit a viral status or could completely crash if the product was just a fad. For the companies that offer services, the social trend is the routine acceptance of that specific niche in the global world. Ford Motor Company, which once traded at less than a dollar, is now a $160 billion-dollar empire.

Political Trends:

A time of political charge in a country affects stocks too. Politicians decide which way the economy and by extension, the businesses will go by erecting policies. These decisions can alter stock markets and they doesn't have to be large changes like presidential elections but can be as small as a county election for small businesses that trade in penny stocks. A good trader keeps in mind the effect political instability can have on the stock direction.

Industrial Situation:

The marijuana industry hit a jackpot as soon as it was legalized in Canada. Similarly, stocks in a coal mining company are continuously declining because of the environmental bills consistently passing in the assemblies all around the world. Keep an eye on the overall situation of the industry your target company belongs to.

Economic conditions:

Even though not as much affecting to penny stocks, economic conditions of the startup base of your targeted company can affect the price to earnings ratio of your stock. A little background research will be helpful. A company from a third world country like Pakistan or India is more prone to troubling economic conditions than a country from an economically stable country.

Competition:

Competition doesn't necessarily mean physical companies that provide similar services or products like your targeted company. This term also encompasses market shares of the company in the industry, market share of the competing companies and the new competition you could expect to have in the industry. The last one is also known as barrier to entry. The more difficult to enter an industry, the lower are the chances of new competition but it's consequently harder for your company to set its foothold in the market. For examples, the automobile industry has already selected its favorite producers. It is very hard for a new company to make its mark in the industry, which is filled with hot shots like Ford, Toyota, Audi, GM and many more. But it is comparatively very easy for a company to make its place in something more volatile or changing. For example, financial technology, companies based on the idea of blockchain put forward in 2009 have seen a rapid increase in public interest and by consequence, their share prices. A market research is required for the understanding of barriers of entry in the market, which can translate to the probability of tackling new competition.

Always prefer high barrier of entry for companies that have established themselves in the market, for example in complicated industries where almost every production is firewalled behind patents and regulated by governments. For a company that is starting to just grow a bud, a low-end barrier to entry is recommended because it's easier to make a place if the monopoly isn't working against you. This includes websites, everyday commodities like toothpaste and soap to restaurants and pizza places.

Analyze competitive advantages: Competitive advantage is when a company outperforms its competitors because of advantage in PESTLE factors: Political, Economic, Socio-Cultural, Technological, Legal, and Environmental or because they have a VRIO (Valuable, Rare, Inimitable, and Organized) resources, unique competencies in what they do or innovative capabilities that are hard to find or invaluable. A company with a patent for a certain process is in extremely advantageous position relative to all the companies that are targeting for similar product. A company in Pakistan or India has a huge upside because of cheap and extremely large labor base.

There's another aspect to competition usually overshadowed. Companies buy shares in rival companies as an effort to hedge their own profits and losses to their rivals. They also do this to create ripple in the stocks of rivals at the time they want to. Checking for shareholders of a company you are targeting is a good exercise to find if the rivals are potentially trying to take over your target company by slowly buying their way to the investor table.

Chapter 14: Making Wise Penny Stock Choices

Penny stocks are volatile and can pose a huge risk in most situations because;

Companies that one is likely to purchase the penny stocks are low profile companies with no big names.

These companies lack track records for one to take into consideration.

They lack sufficient stock or a specific market in some instances.

Predicting accurately the future of these penny stock companies is hard.

Finding a stock broker who works with you and not against you.

Why people flock Penny Stock Markets

People flock Penny Stock Markets because of there exist affordable ways to invest in stocks in a company that is virtually unknown. One ought to keep in mind the following key factors in mind when investing in penny stocks.

Share Structure

This refers to how the stock shares are distributed throughout the shareholders. Take this scenario. You buy a right amount of penny stock that looks splendid to purchase. However, it turns out that one shareholder holds millions of shares of that stock in an offshore account. The problem that arises here is what is going to happen now that you have already purchased the shares. If they are not good people, they will sell off their stock as soon as you invest into the penny. They will do this for a simple reason that the value of the stock will have gone up. Although there exist only two holders, it is more likely that they will decide to sell off their stock shares and in the end, your stock valued drops a considerable amount. In the end, they have managed to sell stock and you are left with something not worth as it looked like in the beginning. If you decide to turn around and share your inventory, the biggest problem you will face is the rise in stock prices making them too costly and risky. The chances are high that you will not be able to sell them off for a profit. To avoid such an incidence, you need to do your homework very well and learn as much as possible on the share structure of the stock. The below-listed points should help you make a wise decision.

Try as much as possible to avoid penny stocks with limited share stocks with few individuals particularly those that are in one stock holders account offshore.

Ensure that the penny stock is spread out and the stock has many stockholders. This can enable you to get a good price for your penny stock.

When taking the share structure into account, be sure to see benefits offered as well as risks involved in the stock.

The Penny Stock Investing Company

When it comes to investment, the first step is to learn as much as you can about the company that you want to invest into. The bottom line is, most likely; the company has not been trading on the stock market, and it is therefore not well known. If you want to invest into a penny stock, you must spend some quality time doing research to develop your strategy to make money with them. However, one of the key challenges is the fact that you are dealing with a company that is relatively unknown. Here are important things to be done before investing in a penny stock company.

Know the business's name, address and phone number from the broker selling them.

Contact the company with the number given.

If you cannot reach the company with the contact provided, find out if there is an alternative phone number or better still try and get another contact online.

If you are unable to find information about the company you want to invest in, consider another penny stock.

Once you can reach the company via a phone call take to ask questions such as; Where are they located and what do they do? What does their client base look like? Be keen to point out things such as how the phone call is being answered, the companies reputation in Better Business Bureau, if the company has factors that play a role on how business can be done better among others. Make sure you can find out information on their customer relations because this gives you an idea of how well your stock will go up. If you discover that the company is having difficulties in giving you the relevant information you are asking, avoid them because any legitimate company will want to do business and providing information should not be a problem.

Learn About the Stock

Taking a look at the stock itself is another critical aspect you should take into consideration. It is important to keep in mind that many stocks will tend to provide you with information on what deal you can get from them when you analyze their history. No matter what investment you are getting in, whether it is penny stock or any other securities you should strive to gather as much information as possible about the stock. This is the only way you can be able to make the right decision concerning that stock since the stock history tends to repeat itself most of the time. For instance, if you notice some splits in the stock this should raise red flags. When you also notice several merges with the stock, this should be something to worry about as it could mean troubles to the company. In general, you should do the following;

Look and analyze the penny stock history.

Find out if the penny stock has had very many reverse splits in the near past or distant future.

Find out if the penny stock has had many reverse mergers. This will give you a clue about the actual trends.

Based on the facts that you find, analyze any risk you believe is involved with the stock.

If the stock you are interested in happens to have several reverse mergers or reverse splits you many consider looking for another penny stock or better still realize the risk involved.

Doing the above-listed things will help you know if it is worth investing your time and resources in a given stock. With just more research time you can find critical information that can save you a significant loss in the future. You are more likely to find solutions and answers to your questions. List down any possible problematic penny stock that you may consider to invest in and make a wise decision.

Chapter 15: The Steps To Success In Penny Stocks

Now, you have come to the part of this book where you will learn all there is to know about starting your penny stock trading venture. You might think that penny stock trading is complicated, with all the rules, things to look out for, complicated stock exchange terms and all that, but it is actually simple. Read the following for the four most basic steps in starting your undertaking in penny stocks.

Research

Just as how you start doing anything that you are unfamiliar with, the first thing you need to do is research. In this book, the term 'research' is used to mean two kinds of research. Before going to battle you must first get your weapon ready, and in the world of penny stocks, there's nothing better than information to be your weapon.

The first is general research. This step involves gathering general information about penny stocks: What it is, how to go about with it and most especially the risks involved. This part is already taught in this book. Through this, you already have the proper knowledge for your general penny stock research.

The second research is the specific stock research. This kind of research should actually be done when you are already looking for prospective penny stocks to invest in. Researching about the stock you are going to invest in should essentially be done when dealing with all kinds of stocks, but this is especially important for penny stocks. That is because, as you can recall from the previous sections, information about penny stocks is quite lacking and harder to find, as compared to other kinds of stocks.

In researching about penny stocks there are two things you need to look for: For one, you should look for any accessible public data about the stock. The second thing you need to look for is information on the stock's historical performance. In looking for this, you have to observe and take note of the kinds of events that occurred and the reactions of the share price. An example of these events is instances when the price of the share remained as it is when there should have been an increase. An event such as this may suggest that investors have looked over the stock's information and decided to steer clear from investing on the stock.

Choose a Broker to Set up an Online Brokerage Account With

As soon as you have done enough research, the next thing to do to start your penny stock investments is to set up your own brokerage account just as you would in a bank. A brokerage account is the platform from where you will be able to buy stocks and other investments. It is also here that your money will be held along with your investments. When you buy shares, your money will be taken out of your account and exchanged for company shares. Then when you successfully sell your shares they will then be converted to money.

There are different kinds of brokerage accounts out there. There are those brokerage accounts that you can manage yourself, but this is not recommended for beginners. For novice penny stock investors like you, it is best to select yourself a broker. These paid professionals will be the ones who will directly buy or sell your stocks as they are told. Of course, you also have to allot them their payment, called 'commissions' or 'commission fees'. These payments can start from as low as five dollars to as high as hundreds.

There are two types of stock brokers that you can choose from: Full service stock brokers known as traditional brokers and discount stock brokers.

Full service brokers offer a much more extensive array of services, including giving you advice and suggestions on what shares to buy and which investment can be more profitable for you. Because of these services, traditional brokers tend to have a higher commission fee compared to discount brokers. Enlisting these kinds of stock brokers is only good for investors who plan to do only a few trades, and can afford to spend a lot of money. If money is a concern for you, hiring a full service stock broker is unadvisable. Commission fees for brokers like them can cost you a hundred dollars for purchasing stocks and another hundred for selling. That doesn't include other service fees.

A good choice for beginner investors would be to employ discount stock brokers. Although they offer a very limited number of services, you have more freedom when it comes to decisions. If you prefer to be more independent in your decision-making process, you should opt to hire discount stock brokers, as their services only include giving limited investment advice. Consequently, their commission fees are cheaper, and you as an investor can save more money.

A much better option for you will be online discount brokers, partnered with an online brokerage account. Using the power of the internet in these times will be to your advantage. Because you will be the one mainly managing your account, and using the internet is the most effective way to do so. Online brokerage systems can help you keep an eye on your account and execute orders to your stock broker. Here, you can see market indexes, monitor buy orders that are open, be updated on quoted stock prices and get access to analyses and researches done by your broker any time you want to help you make your decisions. With this arrangement you can save a lot of money from commission fees, and at the same time make your transactions easier.

When you have finally chosen a broker, setting up your brokerage account will become much easier. You only have to contact your broker(s), and they will provide you with the forms or files that need to be filled out. Most of the time they will be the one who will create the account. Of course, you cannot start an account without an initial cash deposit or a minimum investment. This can range from a few hundred dollars to a thousand. After this, your account will be up and running after approximately three to four days, and you can start investing by then.

Buy

Assuming that you have already set up your brokerage account, the next step is to start buying stocks. This is the most crucial part in the course of all your penny stock transactions. The moment you make a mistake of buying and investing in the wrong stocks, it is right then and there that you are already bound to lose money.

Buying stocks is quite simple. When you want to purchase shares of stocks, you should first contact your broker and execute a buy order. But before doing this, you must first ensure that your brokerage account is stocked up with an adequate amount of money, enough to be able to pay for the share costs and commissions that you will eventually incur.

When contacting your broker, you must have already done your research, and by then have the following set of information: the ticker symbol of the organization that executed the stock, market that the stock is being traded, number of shares or the volume that you want to get, price of the shares that you are prepared to pay and finally, the order's duration or how long you want it to last (it can be for only that specific day or until the date that you selected).

The ticker symbol is the trading symbol with which organizations are identified within the stock exchanges and bulletin boards. For example, you can tell your broker that you want to purchase 1,000 shares of a specific company with a ticker symbol HYPO at 1 dollar or less than that. You can go on to say that the stock is traded on the OTC Bulletin Boards, and you want this order to remain active until Thursday. By this time, what you need to do is wait, and it is up to your broker to deal with the transaction.

So, if ever the price of HYPO shares becomes equal to or less than $1, your broker will purchase the shares. If you check on your online brokerage account, you will discover that you already have 1,000 shares. Consequently, the money in your account which will serve as payment for the shares and for the broker's commission fee will also be transferred to the respective recipients, in this case $1,000 to HYPO and approximently$5 to your broker.

But how can you know if a certain penny stock is a good investment or not? The information can help you answer the question. Four of the things that you primarily need to look out for in a penny stock are the following:

The price range must be from 50 cents to two dollars. Stocks with prices higher than two in the Over the counter Bulletin Board is a bit harder to find.

The daily average volume must be not less than 100,000 numbers of shares. This will be discussed more in the next chapter.

The stocks should be moving higher in the market.

Avoid stocks from companies with negative growth rates in earnings. You can get this information in data released to the public through the SEC or in listings.

Sell

Just like buying penny stocks, selling penny stocks is also very simple, although it is not that easy. As discussed in the third chapter of this book, which talked about the benefits and risks in penny stock trading, finding a buyer for penny stocks is quite difficult. However, having a stock broker to do the actual trading for you will make it several times easier.

As in buying, all you need to do in order to sell your penny stock is do a bit of research, contact your broker and execute a sell order. Also, the information that you gave your broker for your buy order is the same as the ones you will have to give to them for your sell order. These are: The ticker symbol, market, volume of shares you wish to sell, price of the shares and finally, the order's duration.

As an example, you can notify your broker that you want to sell from your account 1000 of your shares in a specific company, with the ticker symbol HYPO. You can then tell them that the stocks are in the OTCBB and that you wish to sell your stocks at two dollars or more, with the order being active until the following Wednesday.

So, if the stock price of HYPO does become two dollars or more, it will be sold. The money that is exchanged with the stock will be transferred to your account, which can then be used for another transaction, but this money will already be deducted with the broker's commission fee. Consequently, you now have $1, 995 in your account.

If you want to know if you had made profits from your transactions or not, you can visit stocks and investment websites to help you gauge your profits, or you can do the computation yourself. To perform this, just simply compare or subtract the money you shelled out for your buy order and the money you shelled out from your sell order. For example, if the buy order cost you $1,005 ($1,000 for the stocks and $5 for the commission fee), and you got $1, 995 for the sell order ($2,000 for the stocks, subtracted with $5 for the commission fee), after subtraction you then have a profit of $990!

Chapter 16: How Stock Screeners Help You Trade Penny Stocks

Search parameters are one of the greatest inventions of the information age. They allow people to set the standards by which they want to look for . . . well, look for just about anything. Stocks are no exception; ergo, penny stocks are no exception. The tool most people use to search for specific stocks is known as a stock screener. There are thousands of stocks to choose from and stock screeners sieve stocks from those thousands down to just one (providing the parameters are tight enough).

In other words, stock screeners save you time and money by locating the penny stocks right for you. If you're only looking for stocks selling between four and five dollars, then that's what you enter into the parameters and, viola: Stocks worth between four and five dollars are the only ones that show-up in your queue.

Like most internet applications, stock screeners can be used for free if you know where to look. Luckily, you don't have to look far as both Yahoo! and Google financial services have versions of the software that you can use at no charge. Better versions of stock screeners will cost you a fee to use – most of the time they're a service of a financial site that charges membership fees. Regardless, even the free stock screeners can streamline your investment searches and are worth the time it takes to use them.

Keep in mind, however, that stock screeners can only read information directly related to the stock.

You're still going to have to do your own research if you want to know something about the companies themselves. So, if you're only interested in buying into companies that don't outsource labor and have a green thumbprint, it's on you.

Having said that, stock screeners are like the pliers of online financial tools – they're not specialized at all, but can give you a solid grip on most of the kind of stocks you're looking for, if the information you want is directly about the stock.

Now you have a rough idea of what stock screeners are, but in order to use them you'll need to know the types of search options available to you. These are based on general criteria that are commonly used when buying or selling stocks . . . the caveat being that you're only going to be using the stock screener to buy stock. You can use a stock screener to help you sell stocks but you'll have to become more familiar with the software to use it for this purpose, and you'll probably need a "pay for use" version to get the kind of detailed info you need to make it worth your while. Below is a list of most of the common search options:

Price

The title says it all – price is the easiest way to screen for stocks, and when it comes right down to it, it's probably the most important. If you're a newbie then this is probably the criteria you're going to focus on, luckily it's one that's user-friendly on all stock screeners.

Market

The exchange a stock trades on is representative of its quality. Bottom of the barrel penny stocks can be eliminated by choosing the market they trade on. It's literally as easy as clicking your mouse.

Industry

This one is especially handy if you know a lot about a particular field. If you work in industrial manufacturing, then it's worth your while to filter your stocks so you're looking at companies you know a little about . . . some knowledge is better than no knowledge. This tool can be particularly effective when combined with the price and market filters.

Activity

A snapshot of a year can be much more effective than looking at a single day's trading. Stock screeners will allow you to look at how a particular stock has performed overtime. This can be something as simple as looking to see if a stock has consistently grown over the course of a given time frame, or something more complex – like assessing the volatility of a stock to see if buying a high risk / big payoff stock is worth the trouble. You may end up using the activity filters more frequently as you become comfortable with the market and you get more adept at customizing the stock screener.

Size

Penny stocks are generally for smaller companies, but how small is too small? You can use the stock scanner to give you the estimate for a company's total value. That way you can decide if the company is big enough for you to mess with.

Just like with any tool, the more you use stock screeners the better you're going to get at using them. One facet of stock screeners that you may have not thought of is that you can use them to help teach you the market. There's nothing about using the tool that says you have to purchase a stock.

So, take your time and play with the parameters to help you spot trends and movement. Stock screeners aren't going to give you the inside tip on frozen orange juice concentrate, but they can show you how companies involved in that industry have been performing over the last twelve months, and with that information you can make an informed decision about how to move in the market.

Chapter 17: To Business - Penny Stocks Basics

These are an amazing range of investment assets that all work towards meeting one primary goal, which is to make money for the investor. One of the assets that is gaining ground is penny stocks. The name implies that you would be investing pennies, however, this is not entirely true.

Penny stocks are investments that are low in price. They may not be as low as a penny, but they are normally lower than $5. Their low values mean that they are not as popular as traditional stocks, yet, they can still give one a handsome return. The reason that many people tend to stay away from penny stocks is because they have been tainted over time with numerous scams and elevated levels of corruption.

There is a simple way to avoid the scams which could cost you your investment.

Before you choose penny stocking, you need to choose a high quality company to invest in. This company will have clear competitive advantages, revenue that is on the increase, a growing market share, barriers of entry that are high for their sector as well as strong fundamentals. To select the right company is no small feat, so you need to find a professional penny stock analyst for help.

Here are some reasons why penny stocks are considered highly risky and cause concern for investors:

There is little information that is availed to the public about these stocks. Investors need to have sufficient information pertaining to every stock that they want to trade in but penny stocks are different. Not many people know much about these kinds of stocks and so, there is no sufficient information that can be used to guide the investors in making the right decisions. The little information that is available to the public cannot be fully trusted because it is not really from credible sources.

Companies selling penny stocks often do not have any history: most of these companies are newly established and so, they do not have a past that investors can check out to determine if they are good enough to invest in or not. Some of these companies are those that are approaching bankruptcy and they are looking for some financial support in order to stay in operation a little longer. It is pretty hard to determine the stability of such stocks because they do not have any reliable history or they already have a bad reputation.

There are no standards in trading penny stocks: most of the credible stocks that are traded in the common stock exchanges have minimum standards that are used to govern them and ensure that investors are getting something at the end of the day, not just the companies. This is not the case with penny stocks. Companies do not have to meet certain requirements in order to stay in the stock exchange and are able to move freely from one small exchange to the other without any issues at all. Investors are therefore risking so much investing in stocks that are not governed by any standards at all.

Lack of liquidity: Penny stocks are the kinds of stocks that do not have much liquidity and this means that they have high chances of not selling again. What business people do at that instant is to lower their prices so that they can seem attractive to some buyers. That is why penny stocks can be manipulated so much in order to benefit a few traders. Wise traders will buy as many stocks when the prices are low only to sell to other investors after a slight increase in the price, for a good return.

Understanding the Key Terms

Once you have received advice from your penny stock analyst, you will be ready to try your hand at trading, though you must be able to understand the terms that you are used. Here are the most common ones: -

OTCBB – This stands for Over the Counter Bulletin Board. This is an exchange where you can trade stocks that have failed to meet the listing requirements of the main exchanges. Companies that trade their stocks in this exchange are usually the small businesses whose future growth cannot be guaranteed that is why investing in these business is considered as highly risky.

Pink Sheets – Over the counter stocks which are not listed on exchanges that are established, such as NASDAQ or the New York Stock Exchange. This is another way through which stocks that do not meet the listing requirements of the main exchanges are traded. The pink sheets do not have any regulations at all.

Bid – This is the price that you are able to sell your penny stocks shares.

Ask – This is the price that you are able to buy your penny stocks shares.

Stop Loss Percentage – This is the highest percentage level that you are willing to risk for a loss

Profit Percentage Gain – This is the highest percentage level that you are willing to take for your profits.

Pump and Dump – This is a strategy that is when trading in penny stocks which someone promotes a stock so that the price can increase and they are able to sell their stock at the higher price.

DTCC: this stands for Depository trust and clearing Corporation. This is the corporation that handles the clearing securities of brokers. It is the body that ensures that brokers are offering the right services at all times, without scamming investors. When you decide to start investing with the help of a brokerage account, you have to ensure that the broker of your choice is DTCC eligible. This way, you will not be highly charged and also, you will have an easier time selling the penny stocks that you will invest in.

The Right Tools and Important Starter Tips

In order for you to be successful at penny trading, you need to have the right tools available at your disposal. To begin with, you must have a computer that is fast as well as reliable. Things change within seconds with penny stocks, and you do not want to miss out on a profit making opportunity. This means that your internet connection should also be fast, with minimal time loading pages and confirming transactions.

While ensuring you have this basic tools, you must pay attention to your security and safety as well. When carrying out financial transactions, ensure that you have a strong password. Avoid day trading while you are on a public connection, and if you have no choice, make sure that you log out of your account as soon as you are done.

As you are preparing your money for the trade, you should deposit it into your account a few days before you will need it.

This is because money often takes a few days to reflect in your account, and to be available for purchasing stock.

Finally, when you are choosing your broker, you will likely select an online broker that handles a host of different assets. You need to confirm whether this broker is friendly towards penny stocks, and if there will be additional fees which are placed on the minimum deposits when trading penny stocks.

Penny stocks can make you a great return, and you should also be aware that they can cost you significant losses as well. Before you move forward, keep in mind the fact that penny stocks are high risk. The penny stock market is highly volatile as even any negativity or hype around a penny stock can radically shift the share price.

For the most part, they are not regulated, which means that if something goes wrong, there is no safety net that will save you. This is also a positive, as it means you can benefit if things go right. To protect your money, you should do some research and establish which sights have received warnings from the regulators, and how much information the site is willing to disclose to an investor. With sufficient due diligence, you will be able to select a site for penny stock trading, knowing that you are making a calculated risk that could have a fantastic payoff.

Although penny stocking is seen to be a form of investment, it is more like a game. When you play a game you have a winner, a loser and a game plan. In order to get to the win, you evaluate every scenario and make calculated decisions. If you make a mistake, you accept that this could cost you the win. What this means is that at any time, the direction that you are taking in this game can change, and even with a loss on the way, you still have the room to make a comeback.

Chapter 18: Penny Stock Faqs

Here are some FAQs (frequently asked questions) on the topic of penny stocks that you need to understand in order to comprehend the topic better.

Are penny stocks good investments?

Yes. Penny stocks are great investments. When it comes to stock market investments, there really is no universal yardstick to measure the value of one investment against another. You have to evaluate each one individually and not generalize about them. Penny stocks are great investment choices if you want something reliable and worthwhile to help you increase the value of your money. They can take in a small sum and cough up a big profit. The key is to understand what stocks to pick and what to avoid.

Will penny stocks add to my existing portfolio?

Yes. Penny stocks will be a part of your existing portfolio. You can diversify your portfolio by investing in penny stocks and avail yourself of its benefits. Although they are priced low, they are still counted as bona fide stock market investments. Penny stocks are classified as company shares just like common or preferred stock. Regardless of how full your portfolio is, penny stocks will add a little "extra" to it and make it a bit more dependable in terms of positive output. So don't overthink the prospect of having penny stocks in your portfolio and add them in confidently.

Should penny stocks be treated as risky investments?

Yes. Not just penny stocks but also all other stock market investments should be considered as risky. As you are well aware, the stock market can throw up both good and bad outcomes. Penny stocks do not enjoy any special privileges when it comes to that and you have to be prepared for anything that might come your way.

Picking the right stocks will no doubt help you but there are no guarantees that it will always work that way. You should prepare for both profits and losses that might come your way.

What is a good sum to invest in penny stocks?

That is entirely your choice to make. Many people start by investing a small sum to see how it goes for then and slowly build up on the value. If you think starting out with just $50 is a good idea for you, then you can consider it seriously. Given that most penny stocks remain within the $5 and $10 range, you don't have to worry about your budget going over-board and $50 can help you pull in a good amount of quality penny stocks. Once that pays off, you can invest in more.

Can penny stocks be transferred?

Yes. Penny stocks can be transferred from one account to another if is mutual consent. Penny stocks are more or less regarded as regular stocks and you can transfer them from one account to another. You can speak with your trader or dealer to have them transferred. It might take a few days for the transaction to be processed and, once done, you will be able to see the details of the stocks in the transferee's account.

Why are penny stocks sold OTC?

OTC or over-the-counter transactions are mostly carried out for all those investments that have small values attached to them. Such investments are not listed on any stock exchange and can only be purchased through a dealer network. Penny stocks, as you know, are valued between $5 and $10, which makes them ideal to be traded over the counter. This system is also known as pink sheets owing to the issuance of pink colored sheets that carry the bid and ask prices. Over the years, the system changed quite a bit and you might not see the same old pink sheets that were once used since mostly everything is now electronic.

Should penny stocks be traded intraday?

Most people prefer to do so. Penny stocks have a lot of volatility and it is best for you to dispose of them within the same day. Doing so will help you prevent unnecessary risks that can plunge your investments into bad debts. That said, however, it might be best for you to hold on to some penny stocks for some time. It is highly subjective and you should make a call on it based on your assessment of the stocks. Try trading in them on an intraday basis and once you get the hang of it, you can start holding your penny stocks.

Is this book a thorough penny stock guide?

Yes. This book can be regarded as a thorough penny stock guide that will help you get started with penny stock trading. It will also allow you to make the right investment choices and improve the state of your investments. You can both diversify your portfolio and correct any past mistakes by investing in penny stocks.

Can I short penny stocks?

Yes. Shorting is an option that is available for any investment in the stock market. Shorting refers to selling a stock that you don't own. You will have to borrow them from someone and then return it to them within a period of time. You, as the person indulging in the short, will wish that the penny stock's prices drop by the time you buy it back and return it. Shorting can pay off very well, provided you pick stocks that are doing well currently but will surely fall in value within a stipulated period of time. But there are risks involved here as well as the shorted stock's price might rise by the time you buy it back to return.

What are some of the risks of penny stocks?

There are many risks involved in penny stocks. For starters, you have to be wary of their volatile prices. It can get extremely tough to predict your penny stock's price changes and it might go from high to low in no time at all. Second, penny stocks are not as easily available as regular stocks. You will have to wait a little before getting the stocks, as your dealer will have to find them for you.

These are the various FAQs on the topic to help you understand it better. Next we will take a look at some of the advantages and disadvantages of penny stock trading.

Chapter 19: How To Get The Most Out Of Penny Stocks

So many people are attracted to penny stock trading today because they do not cost much money and also because there are great chances of making huge returns from them. However, what many traders overlook is the possibility of losing so much money from penny stock investments. Traders with a good amount of money have a wide variety of options to choose from when it comes to investing but for someone with just a small amount of money, the choices are limited and this is where penny stock trading comes in. You have to ensure that you are trading safely at all times and this is the only way you can get the most out of your investment. Here are some key issues that will help you out:

Only focus on penny stocks with a high volume: Investors should be aware of the number of stocks traded in a day and the dollar volume as well. You are better off trading in stocks that sell a good number of shares in a day. A trading volume of about 100,000 shares in a day is a good sign. Trading in stocks that have a low trading volume is a bad idea as it becomes hard for one to get out of their trading position. Also, consider the stock price as this is what determines the liquidity of the shares. You want to invest in stocks that you can easily buy and sell as this is the only way you will make some money in the end, therefore watch out for what is best.

Do not dwell so much on the success stories: There are all kinds of penny stock success stories out there these days and these are used to lure investors to invest in stocks. These stores will be sent to your email, you will come across them in social media websites and anywhere else where business people are sure that potential investors will get to read them. This stories bring out only the good side of penny stocks while the bad side stays hidden. As you know, any kind of investment is full of risks and there are those investments that are riskier than the others. Penny stocks are highly risky; therefore, you have to be careful before you can make the final decision.

Experts will always advice investors to look at penny stocks as something that you cannot really trust. Also, take time to study the kind of stock that you want to invest in so as not to make regrettable mistakes.

Avoid falling for a certain stock: Companies want investors to fall in love with their stocks so that they will be compelled to invest in them. That is why they will use all kinds of stories to divert your attention to their stocks so that you will love them more. Do not allow people to compel you to invest in a certain stock. You have to do your own research first to find out how the stock is and how it has been doing in the past. Choose a stock to invest in according to your needs and investment goals. You will not go wrong if you make your own decisions.

Limit your share size: Many people invest so much money in a stock that they like the most without realizing that in case of a risk, they stand to lose so much money in the end. There are those stocks that promise good returns and one may be compelled to invest more in them. However, always look at the worst side of every situation. What will happen if you want to get out quickly yet you have invested in so many shares? You might have to stick around for a longer time and this means that you will be losing so much in the end. With the swift nature of penny trading, this will clearly be counterproductive for you. Limiting your share size ensures that you are able to get out as quickly as possible when things start going south.

Also, do not trade large positions because you cannot tell for sure what will happen during the trading period. Position sizing is one thing that traders have to be very careful about. Trading large positions is a great risk that beginners should be careful about.

Always read disclaimers: All manner of tips will be sent your way by business people that wants to market their stocks to potential investors and all kinds of promises will be made. This is another area where potential investors fail terribly. Most of these people are paid to market the company, therefore you do not expect them to say anything bad about the business' stocks. You have to dig deeper yourself to know the other side of the stocks before you can finally make the decision. A business will always send you trading tips in order to make you think that it is the best one to invest in. This is always their target, but if you read the disclaimer and understand more about the stocks, you should be able to make the right decision in the long run. Remember, the disclaimer is always there, but it is often written in the smallest possible font.

Never sell penny Stocks Short: Many people will think of shorting their pumped up penny stocks, but this s a wrong move. This is because of the volatility of penny stocks. If you make a mistake and you end up on the other side of the trade, you can lose so much, and this is something that you should avoid by all means. Another thing you should know about penny stocks is that finding penny stock shares that you can easily short can be difficult especially those that can guarantee you a good return. As a beginner, there are certain things that you just have to leave out for the trading experts.

Do not hold for long: The secret behind buying and holding is in order to make more returns than someone that buys and sells off quickly. This will not work very well for you if you invest in penny stocks. With penny stocks, you have to sell quickly for a small profit at a time because there is no guarantee that things will get better after sometime. One thing that you should know about penny stocks is that you can easily make a 30% profit or even a 20% profit after a few days. This is the time to sell, after a few days for something small, instead of waiting for a higher profit that may never come. If you want to trade safely in penny stocks, accept the small profit and move on. So many people lose because of being greedy.

Do not be too trusting: Companies use all manner of strategies in order to lure investors to invest in their stocks. If you want to be safe as you invest in penny stocks, do not be too trusting. First of all, do not listen to the company management. The company will do its best to convince you to go ahead with the investment even when it is not god enough. The intention of many companies is just to get some money to be able to stay in operation and this means that they can create ghost penny stocks in order to raise the amount of money that they require. You have to be careful not to fall into such traps.

Conclusion

I thank you once again for choosing this book and I hope you had a good time reading it.

The main aim of this book was to educate you on the basic concepts of penny stocks, which will help you get started on the right foot, and to provide you with a thorough explanation of the more in-depth and complicated aspects of penny stock trading.

We explored the definitions of the basic concepts of penny stock trading and some more complex ideas and terminologies. We examined the ways in which penny stock prices are determined and evaluated, which factors will impact the share price, and how to carry out an analysis of a company's share price in order to determine which stock is a good investment for you.

We also looked at general and more specific rules and guidelines that you are advised to follow in order to avoid significant losses and hopefully earn a good profit on your investments.

We talked about the different sources of information that will be available to you, including the various kinds of people whom you will likely encounter during your time in the penny stock trading world. We also discussed when you should trust these people and sources and when you should avoid them.

There are many people in the trading industry who are looking to profit off of you. Some of them will do so while also helping you and others will not be concerned about whether or not you make good investment decisions. Knowing who to trust and who to avoid can play a significant role in your investment success.

Now that you have finished reading this book, you have all of the information necessary to start your endeavor into penny stock trading and begin choosing which penny stocks you will purchase.

Penny stocks, as a concept, are not tough to understand and you can start investing in them once you comprehend the basics. Remember to consistently keep yourself educated about the market. A subscription to Forbes or other great trading magazines or newspapers can be of great help, as well.

You can go through this book again if you'd like to know exactly what it takes to invest in the right stocks. Reviewing the key highlights section will remind you of some of the essential aspects of penny stock trading, if you are looking for a quick refresher. Do not hesitate to go back over any section of the book if you feel that you are not clear on a concept, or if you need to revisit an idea to make sure that you are making educated and informed investment decisions.

Once you feel that you are ready, take the leap and start purchasing stocks! We know that the trading world can sometimes seem overwhelming and complicated, but this book has armed you with all of the information that you require to be able to make decisions that will lead you toward profit and away from losses.

Remember to do your research, and always get as much information as you can about a company and its stocks before you decide to invest. A thorough assessment of all available information can make the difference between earning a substantial profit, and incurring a substantial loss.

Once you start investing, you will have to keep track of your expenses to ensure that you are spending within your limit and not going overboard. Always keep in mind your investment plan and your rules for investment, as we discussed in this book. If you stick to these guidelines, you will avoid making a snap or emotional investment decision that you will likely regret down the line.

Remember your goals, and focus on them if you are ever feeling frustrated with your investments and how long it may take to earn a profit. As we have said, there will be times when you will feel discouraged, but this is a normal and common part of trading and investing. It is very rare for everything to go an investor's way. Everyone makes mistakes, but as long as you learn from those mistakes, you will gradually increase your investment earnings.

I wish you luck with your penny stock endeavors and hope you find success.

www.ingramcontent.com/pod-product-compliance
Lightning Source LLC
LaVergne TN
LVHW011937070526
838202LV00054B/4700